LOVE: BONDAGE OR LIBERATION?

Other titles in the UKCP Series:

LOVE: BONDAGE OR LIBERATION?

A Psychological Exploration of the Meaning, Values, and Dangers of Falling in Love

Deirdre Johnson

On behalf of the United Kingdom Council
for Psychotherapy

KARNAC

First published in 2010 by
Karnac Books Ltd
118 Finchley Road, London NW3 5HT

British Library Cataloguing in Publication Data

A C.I.P. for this book is available from the British Library

ISBN-13: 978 1 85575 510 9

Edited, designed and produced by The Studio Publishing Services Ltd
www.publishingservicesuk.co.uk
e-mail: studio@publishingservicesuk.co.uk

www.karnacbooks.com

CONTENTS

ACKNOWLEDGEMENTS

The ideas for this book came out of a series of seminars and workshops that I gave to qualified counsellors and psychotherapists for continuing professional development. I would like to thank Jennifer Ransom and Hilary Parry for initiating the first of these and for their enthusiasm and encouragement. I am also grateful to Laura Henman and Moira Houston, who first suggested that I might write about these ideas, and to the UKCP–Karnac editorial team, whose initiative allowed this suggestion to become a practical reality. My sister, Debbie Johnson, herself a professional in the field, has given invaluable support in reading the entire manuscript and offering many helpful suggestions. Gerry Hughes, SJ, has been of great assistance in helping with the planning of the work as a whole and in helping me hone my thoughts in relation to some of the ideas. I am grateful to Muriel Maufroy, who first introduced to me the little Sufi story within these pages. Above all, I would like to thank my husband, Laurence Hillel, who has so generously encouraged me in my endeavours and whose continued patient support and painstaking help with the references has been invaluable.

Permissions

I would like to thank the following publishers for permission to reprint the material as cited below:

Pan Macmillan, London for the poem "Text", from *Rapture*. Copyright © to Carol Ann Duffy, 2005

The extract from "Looking for your face", from *The Love Poems of Rumi*, edited by Deepak Chopra, published by Rider. Reprinted by permission of The Random House Group Ltd.

Coleman Barks at Maypop Books, for the extract from Chapter 27, *The Essential Rumi*. Translated by Coleman Barks with John Moyne. Copyright © to Coleman Barks, 1995.

HarperCollins Publishers Ltd. for the quatrain from Rumi, *Whispers of the Beloved*, selected and translated by Maryam Mafi and Azima Melita Kolin. Copyright © to Maryam Mafi and Azima Melita Kolin, 1999.

Shambala Publications Inc. for the extracts from *Open Secret: Versions of Rumi*, by John Moyne and Coleman Barks. Copyright © to John Moyne and Coleman Barks, 1984.

ABOUT THE AUTHOR

Deirdre Johnson is a Training Analyst with the Association of Jungian Analysts and a member of the International Association for Analytical Psychology. She has taught counsellors and psychotherapists for a variety of UKCP and BACP training organizations and has led workshops for Continuing Professional Development in many different environments. She has had her own practice for over 25 years. Further work has been within the NHS and in specialist experience with ethnic minorities. She lives in London with her family.

To Laurence, Rowena, and Timothy,
and those others who have taught me about love.
In gratitude.

A note on confidentiality

In order to protect confidentiality, I have drawn on a whole range of stories from my analysands, from friends and family, from cases that have come up in supervision, in workshops, and in tutoring. The names have been changed, as well as any details that could give away the identity of anyone concerned. In the couple of cases where I have quoted a more specific dream or image, the subject had most kindly given their permission and for these I am most grateful.

Introduction

What is this thing: to fall in love? It is an experience that can vex us with the most bewildering of problems and posit the most difficult of questions. As Jung (1961) said of the classical deity of love: "Eros was considered a god whose divinity transcended our human limits", a daimon "whose range of activity extends from the endless spaces of the heavens to the dark abysses of hell" (p. 386). The fact that so many films are watched and so many books are read on the subject, and in such numbers, testifies to our fascination with the subject. *Casablanca* is the best-loved film of all time. *The Bridges of Madison County* is one of the most sold books. The myths and folk tales that speak of love, such as *Tristan and Iseult* or *Eros and Psyche* are told and retold over centuries. The Persian writer, Rumi, is one of the most widely read poets at the moment. I draw on these works, among others, to explore our theme. One of the reasons I have chosen to do so is that these stories reflect what fascinates the collective and so must speak to something archetypal in us.

Much has been written about the "erotic transference"—falling in love within one's psychotherapist—but much less about falling in love outside of the therapeutic situation. I found myself wondering why it is that falling in love with one's analyst or therapist is seen as so valuable while falling in love outside of the sessions can be seen as almost suspect. Of course, the latter can be a defence against the former, but if falling in love is a common experience for many people, how else do we need to understand it? Can it have any value? What is its meaning? Are there any clues to help one avoid the pitfalls that beset the path of a man or woman in love?

Faced with such disturbances when we love "truly, madly, deeply", we might ask ourselves, is falling in love pathology or ecstasy? If passionate love truly is love and can provoke a real self-giving, why can it also provoke the most intense feelings of hate and jealousy, of possessiveness and competition? Does it enlarge or diminish our personalities? Does it lead to bondage and forms of sadism or masochism, or can it lead to liberation? Must it always defy society's morals or can it provoke self transcendence? Is such love blind, or is it, in fact, able to see with an uncanny perspicacity? Does it only lead to pain, or can it lead to any lasting happiness?

To help us begin to find some kind of answer to these questions, we will turn to the various different psychological accounts of the meaning of falling in love that have been produced over the years. There are accounts from classical depth psychology: Freud, Klein, Bowlby, Winnicott, and Jung. There are accounts influenced by the disciplines of biology, anthropology, and the neurosciences. There are accounts that are essentially religious or theological. We will discover that all of these have something to give, especially in relation to different aspects of passionate love. Each account tells us something about what are the pitfalls and what might be the gains from the experience, and each account gives some indications, thereby, of how falling in love might be dangerous or beneficent.

In the first part of the book, I explore these various descriptions of the phenomenon of falling in love and the different narratives of meaning that each contributes. I have sorted these narratives into three categories: those that describe the person in terms of their past (where we have come from); in terms of the present (what we are now); and in terms of the future (where we are going). Having looked at the contributions to our understanding that each of these makes, we arrive at a rich and multi-faceted picture of what might be happening when a person falls in love. Inchoate and extremely primitive feelings from infancy can be aroused; ordinary and yet very powerful human instincts for companionship and for a mate are evoked at the same time, perhaps, as the deepest yearnings for wholeness of which our human nature is capable. It is very important that each one of these accounts is given due weight and allowed to develop our understanding of what might be happening. Each one of these adds something, and yet, after carefully taking each one of these into account, we find that we have not finally said all that we might say.

In the second part of the book I look at what we arrive at when we put all these accounts together. What does this give us in our understanding of passionate love and what can this teach us? Finally, in Chapter Seven, I look at some practical considerations of how to work with these insights.

PART I

A QUEST FOR MEANING: THE DIFFERENT NARRATIVES TO DESCRIBE THE PHENOMENON OF FALLING IN LOVE

(A) What we have been: the first love affair

CHAPTER ONE

The psychoanalytic discourse: emphasizing the intrapersonal

L et us first address the question: why does falling in love provoke such intense, negative feelings, such as jealousy and possessiveness, greed, rage, sadism and masochism, rivalry and competition, and extremes of idealization and denigration? Classical psychoanalysis has provided some explanations. In this chapter, I will explore those theories that emphasize a person's inner world, a world dominated by the workings of fantasy. Effectively, these narratives put an emphasis on a person's disposition or character. Psychopathology is seen in terms of arrested development: a person is "stuck" at a certain developmental stage that has not been fully worked through. The imputation is that the individual has some innate characteristics, such as a weak ego, that makes them susceptible to psychopathology. This account tends towards the nature pole of the nature/nurture debate. We shall start with the contribution to the phenomenon of falling in love made by Freud's psychodynamic theories, and then those made by Melanie Klein. I have selected only those elements of theory that I consider to be useful in our exploration of the theme. Freud, for example, wrote much on the topic, but there is much also that, in my and others' opinion, has not stood the test of time. Those familiar with these accounts must forgive my brief outline.

Freud's contribution

Transference

It was, of course, Freud who first examined falling in love as pathology. In the process of uncovering the dynamics in the minds of patients suffering from "nervous diseases", his new approach of "psycho-analysis", he found that his female patients were falling in love with him. He noted (Freud 1920g): "Patients repeat all of these unwanted situations and painful emotions [related to childhood love affairs] in the transference and revive them with the greatest ingenuity". His ground-breaking insight was that this special case of projection on to the analyst that he termed "transference", rather than simply getting in the way of the psychoanalysis, might actually be used as part of the "cure". This tool, that is, using the patient's transference and the analyst's countertransference, has become one of the cornerstones of psychodynamic therapy.

Projection

In a nutshell, projection is when we put what is inside us on to the outside (introjection is the reverse, when we take inside what is outside). For example, we do not see certain inner feelings, fantasies, or experiences as belonging to us, but as belonging to someone else. We are familiar with the term in the psychotherapeutic setting, but an everyday example would be one in which a negative feeling is disavowed and attributed to another. For example, a teacher, Marie, applies for a promotion within the school at which she works. She and another colleague, Fiona, in the school are not offered the job and it goes to someone outside. "It doesn't upset me too much," she tells a friend who does not have anything to do with the school, "I'm not that bothered myself, but I do feel for Fiona, who I know will feel terribly let down. I really worry how she will take it." It is not inconceivable that Fiona herself might be saying much the same thing of Marie. Freud (1915c, 1920g) sees projection as an essentially defensive manoeuvre where overly unpleasant stimuli are not seen as emanating from within the psyche, but are taken as acting from the outside. In any relationship, we never see the other purely as they are, therefore, but also as we interpret them to be: overlaid to a greater or lesser extent with the elements that we are "projecting" on to them. This image projected on to the other obscures the objective impression of that other and we fail to see them clearly.

We do, indeed, find that at no other time since childhood do we project with such intensity of feeling on to another as when we fall in love. Love, thus, is indeed blind. Do we ever hope again for so much from any other kind of relationship, or feel so let down when it disappoints, as it inevitably and even in ordinary circumstances must? Perhaps at no other time, since our earliest years, are we then also capable of so much hate. Freud (1905d) claimed that our adult romances echo childhood complexes and quotes: "*on revient toujours a ses premiers amours*" (p. 154). The success of the former depends on how well or otherwise the latter have been resolved. That complex, which he came to see increasingly as the being most critical, in both the transference and in adult love relationships, was the Oedipal complex.

The Oedipal complex

Freud claimed that how we are with our sexual partners is highly influenced by the relationship dynamics with the parent of the opposite sex and the extent to which these have been worked through. Since Freud focused especially on the boy's perspective, he termed this complex "Oedipal", after the Greek myth.

The Oedipal complex, put simply, describes a complex that develops between the ages of about two and five in which a boy seeks his mother as an object of (sexual) love and, therefore, sees his father as his rival. The girl, on her part, sees her mother as the rival for her father's love. Each child has to navigate the difficulties of the complex, and each in different ways. We must note, however, that Freud, being a man of his time, saw the female as a male *manqué*. For example, he failed to see how the symptom of penis envy, taken to be an integral aspect of the female "Oedipal complex", might reflect the disempowerment of women at that time.

But, in general, his theory was to view all love triangles (and, indeed, all triads) as based on this fundamental pattern. In practice, it can be found that a repeated pattern of forming or being caught in love triangles can be much dissolved by beginning to analyse the patterns of the childhood relationship to each parent in turn and to both parents as a couple. It is often the case that something from that time remains unfinished; some intense and passionate feelings have not yet been resolved.

The theme of erotic love triangles and their roots in the Oedipal triangle has been taken up to good effect by a contemporary Freudian analyst, Ethel Spector Person (Person, 1988.) Drawing on Freud's insights, she has explored in detail the elements that make up adult passionate love relationships. For the interested reader, she has analysed the subject widely and gives a detailed classification of both the stages of the experience of passionate love and of the various forms it can take. She has illuminative sections on gender difference, and discusses some of the paradoxes inherent in love, to which I shall return (in Chapter Six). Of particular value and relevance, here, is the wealth of detail in Chapter Nine of her book, which deals with the different forms of Oedipal love triangle. Person differentiates two primary versions of the triangle according to the dynamics between the different participants. There is the *rivalrous triangle*, where the lover is competing with a rival for the love of the beloved, and the *split-object triangle*, where a lover has split their attention between two love objects. She explores these versions and other variations of love triangles in terms of various difficulties with the Oedipal complex. For those who find themselves the subject or object of love triangles, or the therapists working with them, I would very much recommend this chapter.

One woman, Alexandra, seemed doomed to repeat a triangular pattern again and again in her relationships. She experienced herself torn between feelings for two very different types of beloved: one reliable, dependable, but somehow less exciting, the other unpredictable but immensely attractive. Love, for her, was thus split into sexual desire and liking: where there was liking there was no desire and where there was desire there was no liking. This split was projected on to two different men. This pattern is an extremely common one and was described by Freud in men who love their wives without desire and desire other women whom they do not love; it can destroy again and again the possibility of committed love. Simply becoming aware of the roots of this split in childhood dynamics can be a crucial first step towards a resolution of the split.

However, Freud's answers to our questions are made problematic by his making several important assumptions. In seeing the links between the childhood "romance" and later love affairs, he tended to work backwards rather than forwards and over-sexualized the child's experience. He based his psychology of women on an uncritical appraisal of their symptoms that did not sufficiently take into account their economic, political, and social position. Also, in viewing the main complex as relating to a late stage of infancy, he missed earlier baby experiences. It is worthy of note, for example, that the style of a woman's adult love relationships can be based on the style of early relationship to the mother. For Alexandra, the reliable, dependable man was modelled on her father, but the exciting attractive one on her much less dependable mother.

We can see from Freud how, if all later loves are new editions of this first childhood text, falling in love can be a means of reliving and reworking unfinished psychodynamics from the past. An understanding of the dynamics behind triangles in passionate love does much to explain the intensity and the power of feelings such as jealousy, rivalry, competitiveness, and that deep, yearning nostalgia that, here, is essentially forgotten childhood longings. Yet, why do passionate feelings have such a primitive, raw quality to them? Why are we driven to hate and greed, to desires which would seem to tend towards the destruction of the love itself, even, at times, to the destruction of the loved one? To answer these questions, we must look to the works of Melanie Klein, who departed significantly from Freud by seeing the most crucial psychodynamics as being rooted in the earliest weeks and months of an infant's life.

Klein's contribution

For Klein, the sheer power of any psychopathology, including psychosis, derives from its roots in primitive, *early* infantile experiences. By focusing on the early relationship between mother and baby, she has given us a greater understanding of primitive defences, first described by Freud, such as splitting, and of the workings of feelings such as envy and guilt, which have an important impact on adult relationships. It is the equation of the intensity of adult feelings with their infantile roots that makes so much sense of the almost psychotic nature of the projections. When someone falls in love, these projections can take on a delusional nature not so very dissimilar to the delusional transferences that occur within therapeutic work with borderline psychoses. It is these baby feelings, all the more intense for being so raw, that can be replayed in the intensity of passionate love. The lover is, indeed, "mad with love"! In revisiting Klein's works with my theme in mind, I found many little gems of insight that I think help us greatly in making some sense of this "madness". For this reason, I have singled out, in more detail, a few key ideas that seem to me to be especially helpful.

The longing for telepathic understanding

It is probably universal for a lover to long to find in a beloved an attuned response to themselves and their needs. Often, this goes even further: they desire in the loved one an intuitive sense of what they need *without their having to articulate this need*. Every therapist who has heard love narratives will have heard the following desire expressed in one form or another: "I wish that she would know what I wanted without my having to ask." At first, this might appear to be an entirely natural request: having someone pick up on what you might need, without you having to spell this out, would seem to be part of the very definition of being loved and, therefore, in many ways, this would strike anyone as a completely legitimate desire. Indeed, as a *hope* it is entirely natural and unproblematic. However, if we look at what happens when this hope becomes an *expectation* and, hence, a demand (conscious or unconscious), we see that the thought becomes: "I should not have to say explicitly what I want from him; if he *really* loved me he would know." And all those who work with couples, or individuals in couple relationships, know that this desire can prevent the very action—the communication of needs—that can help a couple to relate well to each other.

This yearning can be seen as a yearning for "telepathy". Klein (1963) describes it thus:

A satisfactory early relation to the mother implies a close contact between the unconscious of the mother and of the child. This is the foundation for the most complete experience of being understood and is easily linked to the preverbal stage. However gratifying it is in later life to express thoughts and feelings to a congenial person, there remains an unsatisfied longing for an understanding without words—ultimately for the earliest relation with the mother. This longing contributes to the sense of loneliness and derives from the depressive feeling of an irretrievable loss. [p. 301]

Note her description of this as stemming from the closeness between "the *unconscious* of the mother and of the child". So, some degree of a yearning of this kind would seem to be natural (and we shall return to this in Chapter Two), but, when extreme, would indicate a yearning for what one may feel one has lacked as an infant. In practice, I have found this extreme need for an almost telepathic closeness and understanding to be particularly marked in those who have not, in fact, had sufficient experience of the above as a baby. When the dissatisfied lover begins to see that what they want of their beloved in fact relates to what they would have wanted of their mother as an infant, and if, or when, they are able fully to mourn this early loss, they will be more able to refrain from putting the *whole* burden of that on the partner (of course, all love relationships will, and perhaps should, bear a *little* of this burden). Then the relationship will have a much better chance of success.

One highly functioning individual, John, described struggling with this very problem. The woman to whom he was endeavouring to relate was wanting, and able to ask for, more expression of love from him while being aware that he did, indeed, love her. "It just seems so artificial," he said, "to express love if I have been *asked* to do so. It does not seem genuine." It was, to him, as if the fact that he would be expressing love in response to another's request, rather than on his own initiative, itself rendered artificial the very expression of that love. It was as if "one shouldn't have to ask". Underlying his very natural-sounding objection was the less conscious construct that in a loving relationship it should never have to be the case that needs as such are spelt out to the other. And beneath *this* was his own difficulty in expressing, indeed, in even admitting to himself, the existence of any needs of his own. His had been an emotionally undemonstrative family of origin where there had to be quite an amount of guess-work as to what anyone might be feeling or needing. The learning here needed to be that it is not a weak, humiliating, or shameful thing to have needs.

In another situation, the reverse was the case: a woman, Maggie, had a very natural desire for assurance but found this desire hard to trust. However, if she should ask for reassurance from her boyfriend, she tended to undermine the value of what genuine reassurance *was* given to her by thinking that he only said he loved her because of having been prompted. We can readily see that a relationship in which the underlying rules are that one cannot articulate one's needs (since it is believed to be important that they are intuited without having to be expressed) might become one in which *neither partner's needs are met*.

Of course, a second, very simple but important piece of learning here is that expressing one's needs to another is (or must be) a simple request and not a demand. If the other refuses to, or cannot, meet a sufficient number of the other's needs, then the sensible choice here might be to move on. Another woman, Marion, with a deep abandonment complex, was so desperate not to have a relationship break up, even when the boyfriend was satisfying hardly any of the ordinary needs that might pertain to a love relationship, that she simply tried to force herself to be satisfied with next to nothing from him. This was the cause of a great deal of emotional pain.

One useful and very practical question to pose here is this: is the partner fulfilling what is roughly the usual expected role of a girlfriend or boyfriend or partner in our society or the society within which the person is rooted? There is, of course, also the wider question of whether or not the society itself has realistic expectations of what an intimate relationship can provide. But if not, then we must ask: what is going on for the person who is not having those very ordinary and natural needs met? There may be some kind of secondary gain, a theme we will explore later, or it may be that they are putting up with too little. If it is the latter, then an analysis is needed of why they might be letting that happen. All too often, a childhood terror of abandonment is behind this behaviour.

As Klein, in fact, acknowledged, the influential factors can be in a person's early environment. In Maggie's case, her mother had severe pathology of her own which had prevented her from giving her children the reliable attention and consistency that they needed. The pain of not experiencing those basic early needs being met leads so often to a repression of the needs themselves. When such needs reassert themselves, as in the context of falling in love, acute anxiety will be provoked at the prospect of the original pain and humiliation being properly felt.

An image that I have sometimes found useful to describe this idea is that of putting a date stamp on foods. Discovering the original date of passionate feelings and "putting a date stamp on them" allows you to see when they have passed their "sell by" date. It is easier to know which foods need to be tested out and which are safe to keep if we know how old they are. Even when we are not entirely clear about the date, we can be more circumspect about what we are willing to trust as fresh. Thus, in any therapeutic practice, the therapist often finds that it is not so much the case that the client's feelings are not valid but that they are perhaps *no longer* valid; they are left over from an earlier time. For a lover in love to realize that their negative behaviour, which so bedevils them and which they may loathe, stems from baby passions is not only to understand it, but also to perhaps begin to have compassion for the tiny self they become in such moments.

The flight from loneliness and the flight from dependence

In her study of loneliness, Klein (1963) observes how, in some people, the need for the mother is never fully relinquished, and writes,

> Some infants use extreme dependence on the mother as a defence against loneliness, and the need for dependence remains as a pattern throughout life. On the other hand, the flight to the internal object . . . is often used defensively in an attempt to counteract dependence on the external object. . . . The denial of loneliness, which is frequently used as a defence, is likely to interfere with good object relations, in contrast to an attitude in which loneliness is actually experienced and becomes a stimulus towards object relations. [p. 311]

Often, in my work, I find that the very understandable experience of loneliness in a life that is too solitary is being denied. Behind this denial lies a repression of intense loneliness in childhood. When that earlier loneliness is relived and understood, the individual can let him- or herself experience the loneliness of their present lives. As this newly felt loneliness is now experienced as intolerable, they come to have a strong motivation for changing their overly solitary way of life.

Although Klein does not give an explanation in her essay of why this should be so (and we shall explore this later in Chapter Two), this observation can give us some valuable insights in working with those who fall in love and use extreme dependence on the lover as a defence against loneliness. Of course, one can see the reverse: Klein (1952b) notes that, faced with a multitude of anxiety situations in a relationship, "the ego tends to deny them and, when anxiety is paramount, the ego even denies the fact that it loves the object at all. The result may be a lasting stifling of love" (p. 73).

For example: a man, Peter, who seemed quite capable of love, found that with his girlfriends he would at times lose all sense of loving at all. The acute anxieties that the relationship evoked led to an automatic, and, therefore, not consciously willed, numbness to all loving feelings. At first, he thought the problem lay only in the relationships; once he began to think it might be in him, he could slowly begin to let himself access his own feelings of love in a safe environment.

Klein (1957) cites other reasons for stifling love, many that relate to a person's difficulties in tolerating ambivalence. Ambivalence, here, is a technical term meaning the coincidence of both pleasant and unpleasant feelings. Depth psychology holds that no feeling exists without some degree of the opposite feeling also being present, even if not conscious. Thus, Klein describes how love may be stifled and hate intensified when there may be the pain of guilt at combined love, hate, and envy (p. 219); when there is fear of dependency on mother, and of one's own destructive impulses (p. 223). But one motive above all recurs in psychotherapeutic work. Klein notes this: "In an adult, dependence on a loved person revives the helplessness of the infant and is felt to be humiliating" (p. 223). Again, she does not elaborate on why the helplessness of the infant, revived by dependence on a loved person, should *necessarily* be only painful or difficult, as implied, nor does she explain why this helplessness should necessarily be felt to be humiliating.

A certain amount of dependence on a loved person in adulthood, as in childhood, could be felt also as something lovely, especially, but not exclusively, where that dependence is reciprocal. Dependence on a loved figure, such as a mentor, for example, could be felt to be very positive. Nor does Klein explain why this should be felt by some to be so crippling, and we shall return to this question later. But it is indeed the attempt to avoid feelings of humiliation that drives so many people to deny their need of another.

Here, it will suffice for me to suggest that what precisely is experienced as humiliating and, therefore, insupportable is the having of a need *and the felt experience of the response to that need being actively and voluntarily withheld*. If the beloved indeed knows that their lover has a deep need for them, yet persists in withholding any response to that need, the needy lover may well experience the beloved as having a cruel power over them. But we must note that it can be an easy matter to project on to the other at least three different types of condition that do not, in fact, hold true: first, that the loved one is *aware of the need* in the first place, or, at least, the extent or intensity of the need, second, that they are in general *able to meet that need*, and finally, that they *should* respond in the particular way required. In practice, many obstacles might alter the conditions: the loved one may not realize the existence of the lover's need, or, at least, not be aware of its extent or intensity; they might be unable, rather than unwilling, to meet it, that is, they might be just as helpless themselves, by virtue of their own pathology, as is the lover; and, last, they might, either rightly or wrongly, judge that a particular need is not, in fact, what the lover actually needs.

For example, sometimes it can be the case that we judge that we have a need for a particular response from another when, in fact, that response might not actually meet the underlying need. A particular need, such as the need for love, will stem from a given human instinct, but our learnt methods of procuring love might not be very effective. There is the example of the person who, when sad, tends to talk obsessively around and around their sadness without ever really getting any nearer to the feeling itself. This behaviour might even be an unconscious way of *avoiding* facing what they feel, although consciously they think of it as precisely *the* way to reach their feelings. Thus, they may not need to *talk* more, but to *feel* more and talk less. Their partner might intuitively sense the rightness of not simply colluding with the talking defence with-out realizing how else they might be able to help. All psychothera-pists are familiar with those times in a session when the talk in the "talking cure" is really a defence against the "cure". Between couples, it is often the existence of a mutual and dovetailing pathol-ogy, a "couple match" in a mutual inability to deal well with emotions and emotional needs, that prevents two people from reci-procal giving.

Greed

Relevant to our theme is Klein's exploration of what she terms "greed" (Klein, 1952b). She notes that anxiety about losing the loved object tends to increase greed, which is then felt to be destruc-tive of the external object, and so the ego increasingly inhibits instinctual desires. This process can seriously affect love relation-ships (p. 73). Klein (1957) defines greed as "an impetuous and insa-tiable craving, exceeding what the subject needs and what the object is able and willing to give", and relates it to the original infantile impulse to scoop out, suck dry, or devour the mother's breast. This form of taking in the good destroys that good. It is a form of destructive introjection (p. 181) and we know well that greed can be so impetuous that the good taken in so voraciously cannot be properly enjoyed. However, I suggest that an important distinction must be made between a craving that exceeds "what the *subject needs*" and one which exceeds what "the object *is able and willing to give*". Klein, here, conflates this distinction. For example, a mother too depressed to maintain eye contact while feeding or holding her baby is likely to cause a craving for intimacy that could scarcely be defined as greed in the baby, although when that child becomes an adult it is highly likely to judge such a need in precisely this way. And, due perhaps to a clinging behaviour that has evolved for the same reason, others, too, are likely to judge this as greed. I have had many analysands say of their love relationships, "I am just too needy", by which they mean something very like "greedy". An important task is to discover where that construct originally came from: "You are too needy *for whom*?" When a therapist asks this precise question, the answer can be extremely instructive and even liberating. The superego judgement may have been set up and internalized from the behaviour of a parent who quite simply was unable to cope with an ordinary baby's demands and may, therefore, even unconsciously, have taught their child that he or she was not simply "too much" for them, but too much for anyone.

One very common example in love relationships of a defence against what might be judged as greed is the lover who defends against their need for the other and against any imputation of "greed" by taking control of ending the relationship. There may even be a pattern of always finishing the relationship first or coming across as cold when they are quite the opposite. Consciously, they will judge this as a good way of not seeming to be "too clingy", but, at a deeper level, they are afraid of the intensity of their need for the other. They will be very careful not to let this intense need show. I have known of instances where this pattern was so extreme that the object of such intense passion was actually unaware of being desired at all!

It may be, therefore, an unbearably intense need that has been unfulfilled that provokes the anxiety that Klein sees as increasing "greed", but the behaviour might better be seen as a defence against the sheer intensity—the voracity, if you like—of desire. Indeed, "voracious" is a very apt term, because it does not necessarily imply greed. We can see that this is the case in the sentence: "Exercise left her with a voracious appetite", and, interestingly, the root of the word "voracious", from the Latin *vorare*, is "devour". This takes us very neatly back to Klein's insight about the infantile roots of this kind of need: the baby's desire to devour the mother.

However, it is worth noting that, in this sentence, it is the *appetite* that is devouring, all consuming, and not the *subject*. One woman, Helen, experienced such a hunger for expression of love from her lover that she was in danger of finding even the loveliest of exchanges never enough. The intensity of this "greed" was overwhelming, and she could see that it threatened to spoil a positive relationship. When she explored the quality of the feeling and its roots in raw emotions from her infancy, in which there was considerable neglect, she was able to recognize where the devouring need came from and to take responsibility for when it arose in the relationship. This often seems to be the case: the primary experience is of unmet needs in childhood, creating an intensity of desire that devours or threatens to devour the baby, rather than an innate greed, whereby the baby devours the mother. A person may experience being *devoured by their needs* or find this possibility so threatening that they have learnt to deny such needs altogether.

Falling in love, and the unleashing of desire that this provokes, can throw a person back into that baby intensity of need where there is no memory, no language, and no context with which to temper the agony of a need that has never ceased to gnaw away inside and which has persisted unsatisfied until awakened in its full force.

Splitting as a defence

Klein's exploration of splitting as a primitive defence against ambivalence is so well known that it shall suffice simply to describe it briefly and highlight how it might be employed as a defence in the area of passionate love. Writing about the earliest form of anxiety, Klein describes how, in the baby, in the first three or four months of post-natal life, internal aggression evokes fear of retaliation, giving rise to persecutory feelings. In other words, the baby's own anger at the mother is projected on to the mother and then feared as a possible attack by the mother on the baby. Difficult experiences, both within and without, compound each other and the infant directs its destructive impulses, hate and feelings of persecution, towards what it sees as a "bad" aspect of the mother, while love and feelings of gratification are directed towards the good aspect of the mother. The baby cannot experience the internalized mother as a whole object, and, therefore, splits her into opposing part objects: the good and the bad breast. A particular instance of splitting, which is central to our theme, is idealization.

Idealization

Klein sees idealization as an extreme form of defensive splitting. It is, of course, common knowledge that idealization occurs in the first full flush of love and that it can get badly in the way of a love relationship developing any further. One instance of this might be when the lover feels the beloved to be so far above them as to be beyond reach and, therefore, they do not even think to try ("faint heart never won fair lady"). Or else, the lover might fear the ensuing disillusionment so much that they cannot bear to realize their love and prefer to keep it preserved unsullied, as if in aspic. Or, it might be that the lover reacts with so extreme a disillusionment after the "honeymoon period" that adoration is turned into contempt. For these reasons, it will be of value to explore the theme of idealization at some length.

At this point, I will confine myself to the psychodynamic/object relations approach. Klein (1952a) writes, "The infant's relative security is based on turning the good object into an ideal one as a protection against the dangerous and persecuting object" (p. 49). In other words, once the love object has been split as above, the bad must be prevented from attacking the good; the bad is denied, leaving the good to become idealized. Hence, she goes on to suggest (Klein, 1952b) that idealization is based on denial. "Idealized figures are developed to protect the ego against the terrifying ones" (p. 241). In the context of passionate love, idealization of the beloved might involve the creation of a fantasy of an "Ideal Other", a Miss, or Mr, Right, who can never disappoint. Indeed, this would seem to be an explicit stage in even an entirely healthy experience of falling in love. Since this is so, one might wonder what else this process might serve beyond the immediate, defensive relief from persecutory anxiety. I shall return to this question in Chapters Five and Six.

As Klein shows (1963), in normal psychology, since the beloved can never meet perfection, disillusionment must ensue: "The realization that the good object can never approximate to the perfection expected from the ideal one brings about de-idealization: and even more painful is the realization that no really ideal part of the self exists" (p. 305).

But she has earlier described (Klein, 1957) an extreme, that is, pathological, version of this:

> A very deep split between the two aspects of the object indicates that it is not the good and the bad object that are being kept apart but an [extremely] idealized and an extremely bad one. So deep and sharp a division reveals that destructive impulses, envy, and persecutory anxiety are very strong and that idealization serves mainly as a defence against these emotions. [p. 192]

As we know, Klein sees the integration of love and hate, in other words, the achieving of ambivalence, as a healthy development in the baby at around the second quarter of the first year. She terms the achievement of this stage the "depressive position", since it is opposed to a manic, omnipotent defence. This she would see as being true for all infants, but when very strong splitting and, thus, idealization is maintained in later life, the idealized object can easily turn into its opposite pole, that of the persecutor (*ibid.*, pp. 192–193).

It is very typical of those who love in an extremely idealized fashion for idealization to turn quite quickly to disparagement. Since, in this instance, love and hate cannot be felt *at one and the same time for one and the same object*, the lover experiences either intense swings between these two states at *different times* but with respect to the *same loved one*, or extremes of feelings operating at the *same time* but with respect to two *different loved ones*. Every therapist, at one time or another, has experienced examples of the first in extreme swings in the transference: they are loved or idealized at one point and hated or disparaged at another. I have often found swings occurring in alternation from one session to the next, some-times continuing to alternate in this way in sessions for a long while. Sometimes, a person shows this split with respect to a single, regular girlfriend or boyfriend. In other words, the regular girl- or boyfriend is viewed at certain times as ideal and at other times as useless: it is as if the lover is describing two entirely different people. Or else, as examples of the second case, someone might idealize the latest boy- or girlfriend and disparage earlier ones. Thus: "Sally is so different from my ex, not like any of the others I've been with." Sometimes, we see the situation in which a client manifests *both* types of splitting: at one point, earlier love objects are idealized and the current one is made into "the bad one". For exam-ple: "I should never have left Mike: he really appreciated me. Not like David, who always takes me for granted." Then, at another point, the earlier love objects are disparaged when the current one is experienced as "the good one". Then we hear: "David is wonder-ful; he has such a sense of humour, not like Mike, who could be so dull." The order may then be reversed once the current boy- or girl-friend is seen as bad again. These are all examples of an inability to tolerate ambivalence where both love and hate are felt at the same time for the same person.

Of course, the classic version of this split in ordinary life is the Good Lover/Bad Spouse scenario. And it might be the case that only when the Bad Spouse is left and the Good Lover married that the subject realizes that they have thereby actually turned the Good Lover into the Bad Spouse. It is a pattern that Shakespeare recognizes so perceptively in *Anthony and Cleopatra*. Cleopatra fears that her married lover, Anthony, could become unfaithful to her, just as he has been to his wife, Fulvia, in his and Cleopatra's affair. In Act I, scene III, she asks him: "Why should I think you can be mine and true . . . / Who have been false to Fulvia?" What madness to be entangled with vows "which break themselves in swearing!" Without insight and rightly-directed effort, this process can be repeated over and over and over again.

Klein (1952a) gives us a very good description of what must happen in the analysis of such a person in order for a healing of the split to take place:

> It is only by linking again and again (and that means hard and patient work) later experiences with earlier ones and *vice versa*, it is only by consistently exploring their interplay, that present and past can come together in the patient's mind . . . When anxiety and guilt diminish and love and hate can be better synthesized, splitting processes—a fundamental defence against anxiety—as well as repressions lessen while the ego gains in strength and coherence; the cleavage between idealized and persecutory objects diminishes; the phantastic aspects of objects lose in strength. [p. 56]

What all of this implies, she continues, is an integration of unconscious phantasy that enriches the personality. Of course, Klein is explicitly referring to the healing possibilities within the patient's transference, but my argument is that, as therapists, we should not miss the opportunity to use the healing possibilities of the patient's projections on to a love object *outside* of the analysis. Given the rightful importance attached to transference and countertransference phenomena within the therapy, we can miss the fact that what Klein describes above can still take place even when the love object is not the therapist. I will revisit the theme of idealization again at a later point (in Chapter Four, pp. 101–110).

Narcissism

Klein sees this process of splitting good and bad, whether it is the good (the ego ideal) or the bad that is projected outwards as narcissistic in nature. In the grandiose version of narcissism, depletion is projected outwards on to others and plenitude retained, and in the inverted form of narcissism this is reversed. In the process of falling in love, one can see how easy it is for two people with these styles of relating to be attracted to one another. Judith Pickering, an analyst and couples' therapist, writes in detail about such arrangements (Pickering, 2008.) Drawing on later self psychologists, she returns to the myth of Narcissus to talk of the two ways of relating in terms of Narcissus and Echo. One person is the admired one, and sees their qualities reflected in the adoring gaze of their admirer. The other, as admirer, sees the image of how they would like to be reflected in their adored one. In the particular situation of falling in love, which can be rife with these forms of idealization, the beloved can easily become a repository of one's inner, but denied, sense of depletion or of one's inner, but denied, sense of riches. It is a mistake, however, to think that these roles are fixed, they function as a dynamic and can be reversed, and Pickering gives some excellent examples of how one can also find Echo–Echo, Narcissus–Narcissus pairings (p. 161). In each case, however, what each member of the pair has in common is narcissistic pathology, where self-esteem is lacking and a core inner emptiness dominates. Each yearns to be seen, but neither, in fact, is able to see the other. Instead, their gaze is turned within towards the injury (real or imagined) "of not being beheld in the loving lights emanating from the gaze of the mother's eyes" (p. 152). Where narcissistic wounding is mild, two lovers might well be able to give each other what each feels to be missing; where it is extreme, it is unlikely that either can form a satisfactory relationship without the pathology being worked upon and one or other or both being helped to see themselves and be see and be seen by another.

Bliss

Finally, and closely related to our theme of idealization, let us take a brief look at what we may term "bliss". On this subject, Klein, along with Freud, sees specific parallels between early infant relationships and later love relationships (Klein, 1952c). However, she asserts (Klein, 1957) that the bliss experienced in being suckled is not the basis of sexual gratification alone (Freud), but of all later happiness, and such experiences make possible the feeling of unity with another person; such unity means being fully understood, which is essential for every happy love relation or friendship. At best, such an understanding needs no words to express it, which demonstrates its derivation from the earliest closeness with the mother in the preverbal stage. [p. 188]

I want to return later to this theme of bliss, so, for now, I shall content myself with highlighting two points from the above extract. First, Klein asserts that this bliss is the basis of all later happiness, and specifically the particular happiness involved in a feeling of unity with another person. Second, that, in common with other psychoanalysts, she sees this as relating to deposits laid down in childhood.

Klein's theories can go a long way towards explaining why feelings for a loved one can be so polarized, why love can so easily turn to hate, and why there can be felt to be so little security even where one is loved. It is because these feelings evoke ones that are preverbal, carrying all the intensity of unprocessed primitive states of infancy, that the experience of falling in love can be so fraught.

Although Klein makes mention of the influence of the dysfunctional environment, she does not, to my mind, emphasize sufficiently how this contributes directly to extremes of negative feeling. There is, thus, a danger that a person suffering such extremes within a passionate relationship might be encouraged to examine their infantile experiences of rage against the mother, envy of her riches, jealousy of a sibling, and so on, while not examining enough what might have been dysfunctional in the upbringing that could have brought about an exacerbation of these feelings. We have seen how dependence is still viewed as infantile (no notion of mature dependency, which we will explore later in Chapter Three), and we have seen how greed has been defined not only as wanting more than is needed, but even as wanting more than can be given. I suspect this was due to Klein's ambivalence about quite how far she should depart from Freud. She was more original than perhaps either she or her followers at first realized. One can work through these passionate, intense baby experiences, but, unless there is also some objective assessment of the quality of the early maternal environment, the analysand might still hold on to their defences of self-blame (masochism), repression of hope (depression), and so on. We will explore this further in the next chapter.

The benefits of passionate love as described
by the psychoanalytic narratives

We have seen, in our exploration of some of psychoanalytic theories about falling in love, what are some of the very real dangers
that threaten the formation of healthy relationships. What can these
tell us about how falling in love may be beneficial? Psychoanalytic
narratives give us a real insight into the parental complexes influencing adult love relationships and, thus, why the latter can have
such power, intensity, and conditioned quality. Triangular relationships, especially, can be understood and better dealt with when
their Oedipal roots are disentangled. The obsessive quality of
passionate love can be better understood, and also the factors that
can so readily wreck the formation of effective, satisfactory love
relationships. Hence, what might seem like a negative fate in an
individual's love relationships can be seen to be due to the effects
of unresolved mother–infant, and later, Oedipal, issues. Psychoanalysis has shown that these can, with a great deal of hard work,
linking the past and present again and again, be resolved.

If the damage is such that it is more than a person can put right
on their own, then psychotherapy may well be indicated. That is, if
the negative complexes are preventing the formation of good relationships in the first place, then analysis, or in-depth psychotherapy
work, may well be needed, and may well require work with the
transference and countertransference issues of intense love and
hate, so that ambivalence might be better tolerated. The experience
of passionate love may only be possible at first within the relatively
safe container of the therapy itself. However, later, when it is found
that the therapist survives the hate (and love!) and that love and
hate can coexist, then the subject may begin to allow love to occur in
those situations outside of the consulting room, where love might be
not only felt and acknowledged, but also acted upon. We know that
Freud cautioned against the patient's flight from the exigencies of
love for the analyst, which he termed *acting out*, but, in his day,
analysis was considered long if it was over six months or so. A
patient who is expected (consciously or unconsciously) by their
therapist to wait the full period typical of a contemporary analysis
before such an "acting out" may well find that time has run out on
them. This may well adversely affect women more than men, for
whom it could become, biologically speaking, too late to have a

child. During a long analysis, it is not only the consulting room clock that keeps on ticking.

Again, at first, a new love relationship that blossoms for a client during the course of therapy may need careful monitoring in the therapy to ensure that the complexes do not undermine its chances of success. In time, however, step by step, it may become possible for the client to internalize this monitoring to the degree whereby they can take charge of the way in which the intense feelings from childhood undermine present relationships. By accepting such feelings, and allowing for a catharsis of them, knowing that they stem from the past, they can be given their rightful place.

Thus, the application of psychoanalytic theory or theories can point us to of one of the great values of falling in love and the benefit that it can bring. The compulsion to repeat, first recognized by Freud, can give us the opportunity to rework our first editions and rewrite the script, so to speak. Then the love tragedies of one's life may be transformed from a *Romeo and Juliet* to something more like *A Comedy of Errors*, or an *All's Well that Ends Well*. This work, which, like art, involves reflecting upon emotions in tranquillity, can counter the negative effects of the impulsivity provoked by the intense emotions involved. A careful analysis (by oneself or, if need be, with a therapist) of the pathology involved can slowly unpick the tangle of unproductive dynamics and sufficiently free the natural instinct for love so that it can work well enough to be getting on with.

Why the psychoanalytic narratives are not enough

The limitations of the psychoanalytic discourses have been, at least historically, to do with the fact that, although theoretical acknowledgement of the influence of the early environment is asserted, in practice they concern themselves, not entirely, but almost exclusively, with the patient's inner world. Both the natural need for, and the influences of, others is minimized, and, hence, also the extent of the reparative work that can be done on environmental damage. In looking at the intrapsychic childhood roots of adult love relationships, we have not said all there is to say. Human beings are very much social beings even in childhood and, we now know, even in infancy, and we need to explore falling in love as a phenomenon that relates to the growing infant's social needs and instincts.

CHAPTER TWO

The relational psychologies discourse: including the interpersonal

W e may ask, if the story of falling in love can be bedevilled with intense negative fantasies and feelings, how is it that such negative dynamics are set up in the first place? The various relational psychologies address the problem of the limitations of an overly intrapsychic approach. There is a very real need for others, in babyhood, in childhood, as well as in later life. There are mature as well as infantile dependency needs, and the influence of others, including any siblings, other relatives, or other carers, and even peers, in early life, can be considerable. Jessica Benjamin gives an excellent critique of the limitations of psychoanalysis in so far as it deals only, or too one-sidedly, with the internal world of fantasy and not with relationships to the outer world (Benjamin, 1988). A balance between what may be termed the intrapsychic and the interpsychic, or interpersonal, dimensions needs to be maintained.

Klein, as we have seen, did at least acknowledge the influence of the environment on children but did not elaborate on what exactly those influences might be or how they might affect the child. Although Jung explicitly criticized the one-sidedness of Freud's approach, and his own psychology was very much relational, he did not explore much to do with child development. Later practitioners, such as Bowlby, Ainsworth, Winnicott, Stern, and others used infant observation or formal research studies to discover how best to treat or prevent the ill effects of the environment on children. I will restrict my exploration to those particular influences that relate most directly to the experience of passionate love. Some of these seem to be so particularly relevant to the state of being in love that it will be worthwhile to begin with these.

Winnicott's contribution

Love as mirroring

We touched on the theme of mirrors briefly in looking at narcissistic pathology (see also Schwartz-Salant, 1982), but in the ordinary experience of passionate love a key feature is the loving glance. One of the surest signs of being in love must be the amount of time spent looking at the beloved. If the feelings are reciprocal, then each will look often and deeply at the other. John Donne, one of the metaphysical poets writing in the seventeenth century, uses mirroring as an image of true reciprocity. His love poem "The Good Morrow" (Donne, 1971) is a very accurate description of the kinds of feeling lovers have when they are mutually in love. In the poem, Donne tells his lady, "My face in thine eye, thine in mine appears . . .". The sense of mutual giving and receiving is beautifully conveyed in the repeated internal rhyme and the exact symmetry of the line. There was a particular conceit from that time that two lovers could together produce "looking babies": the image of oneself in the other's eye, and of the other's self in one's own denoted a metaphysical form of reproduction parallel to, but transcending, the physical, sexual form of reproduction. In the latter case, rather than a physical child, the soul as a homunculus, or "little man", is thus born.

How interesting it is, then, that Winnicott employs the image of the mirror when delineating the childhood roots of intimate love (Winnicott, 1967). Working as a paediatrician with an ordinary population of mothers and children (i.e., outside of the field of mental health), he showed a much more detailed understanding of the influence of the early environment on the developing child. He explored both the healthy aspects and the pathologies of what he himself termed the "love affair" between mother and baby.

For Winnicott, the good enough mother acts as a psychological mirror to the baby. When the baby looks at its mother's face it sees itself (*ibid.*). "In other words, the mother is looking at the baby and *what she looks like is related to what she sees there*" (*ibid.*, p. 112); her expression mirrors the baby's mood. In a phrase strikingly similar to Donne's descriptions of what happens in reciprocal love, Winnicott writes that the mother gives "back to the baby the baby's own self" (*ibid.*, p. 118). When the mother cannot respond to the baby, the latter does not get back what he or she is giving, and two consequences ensue: first, the baby's creative capacity begins to atrophy and it looks for other ways of getting something of itself back from its environment; second, when it looks at the mother it does not see itself reflected back, only the mother's face. This face is not then a mirror and the two-way process of exchange with the world does not take place. Some babies, then,

> tantalized by this type of relative maternal failure, study the variable maternal visage in an attempt to predict the mother's mood, just exactly as we all study the weather. The baby quickly learns to make a forecast: "Just now it is safe to forget the mother's mood and to be spontaneous, but any minute the mother's face will become fixed or her mood will dominate, and my own personal needs must then be withdrawn otherwise my central self may suffer insult". [*ibid.*, p. 113]

We might wonder how much of the current preoccupation with self image, as revealed in men's and women's aspirations to fitness or beauty, might not be some form of attempt to reflect back to oneself a positive image relevant to this early stage. One studies the literal mirror as a displacement for the thwarted attempt to study the mother's face and find there what was never there before: a reflecting mirror in which to see oneself (one's self).

It can be seen from this how the child may then learn to be hypersensitive to another's mood and develop heightened antennae in order to be able to pick up every conceivable variation in it. In this pathology lies the making of many a psychotherapist! It can also be seen from this how the person will grow up holding their needs in abeyance, always on the alert for when they should withdraw any demands. This watchfulness can make for a state of anxiety so pervasive and continuous that it seems like an "existential anxiety", a continuous state of dread, part and parcel of a person's very existence, and which is assumed to be the case for everyone. Yet, we find that this particular dread is not a necessary condition of existence: it is just that it was set up too early in life for the person to have been able to note its onset.

With one woman, Madeleine, there was something about the way she held herself that suggested the picture of a child too fearful to let its body relax and to let go, as if she had constantly to "pull herself up by her own bootstraps". There was an impression of a child who had never really felt safely and thoroughly held, so that even when the experience later became available, she still kept herself in check unconsciously. The mother had been inconsistent in her behaviour to her child, who had grown up unable to trust herself at the deepest level. After long years of work on herself, this sensitivity could be usefully employed in becoming an excellent therapist.

If there is no or next to no possibility of an attuned response to her child on the mother's part, then the latter becomes predictably disappointing and the child gives up hope altogether. As the child becomes an adult, a reciprocal, attuned relationship will not even be believed to be a possibility. By contrast, in Donne's description of reciprocal love, the lover explores the beloved's face and finds there his or her own self given birth to, in a mutually creative endeavour. In general, Winnicott (1967) sees a historical process taking place in the individual, which goes.

> When I look I am seen, so I exist.
>
> I can now afford to look and see.
>
> I now look creatively and what I apperceive I also perceive.
>
> In fact I take care not to see what is not there to be seen (unless I am tired). [*ibid.*, p.114]

In other words, the baby feels itself to exist since it is seen by the mother. This allows the infant to become a subject who can look at and see the mother in its own right. Thus, a creative act can happen whereby looking becomes an active event and the internal constructs, or set of ideas, around "mother" that imbue the notion "mother" with meaning (apperception) match with the data of the actual mother, taken in by the senses (perception). There is congruence between the inner and the outer worlds. Projections in all but exceptional circumstances will not (unduly) distort reality.

Psychotherapy is a complex version of this process; it is not

> making clever and apt interpretations; by and large it is a long-term giving the patient back what the patient brings. It is a complex derivative of the face that reflects what is there to be seen . . . if I do this well enough the patient will find his or her own self, and will be able to exist and to feel real. Feeling real is more than existing; it is finding a way to exist as oneself, and to relate to objects as oneself, and to have a self into which to retreat for relaxation. [p. 117]

Adult love affairs can be understood much better if we see the relationship of baby and mother as the "first love affair". Of course, in many ways, such language is imposing an adult perspective on to an infantile one and this can be misleading. But it demonstrates the crucial link between the two and, if we reverse the chronology, we can say that this extraordinary, and yet, of course, so commonplace, bond between mother and child is the prototype of all later love affairs. The adult love affair does not so much hark back to as develop out of the childhood one. This is an important departure from Freud, who insists that the mother has to be *relinquished* as an object of desire rather than *assimilated*.

If that first love affair was unreciprocated for the infant, then later loves for the child, now grown adult, will be similarly unreciprocated. If it consisted in the need for a constant adaptation of self to other in order to fend off abandonment, this style, too, will be the tenor of all later relationships. If the baby was allowed to tyrannize as a little god over the mother, that, too, is likely to be the pattern with intimate others in later years. For Winnicott, for good or ill, our first love affair is with our mothers, and that will do much to determine all later love affairs until or unless the influence of negative conditioning is lessened by the release and integration of feelings, especially hate and love. He emphasizes in particular the experience of the first few months of life as being crucial in laying down the primary pattern for later loves.

Love tokens as transitional objects

A second theme from Winnicott that I would like to draw on for our purposes is that of transitional objects and transitional space. Winnicott knew, from observation, how infants use their fingers or thumbs or fist to suck on, and how later they often attach to a soft toy or piece of cloth (Winnicott, 1953). This first "not-me" possession (transitional object) begins with the above auto-erotic phenomena and extends to the treasured toy. A sufficiently responsive mother will be finely attuned to her baby's needs, so that the baby will not know if the breast has appeared because he or she made it appear or if it appeared of itself. The question: is this object (the breast, or later, the toy) me or not me; is it real or imagined? is allowed, therefore, to remain unanswered. Transitional phenomena have to do with the intermediate space between inner and outer worlds, between self and object, between reality and imagination, between the "me and the not-me". This intermediate realm of experience, the interface between outside and inside, Winnicott termed "transitional space". We can see the vital importance of the existence of transitional space to other activities that span both inner and outer worlds, such as play in children, and playfulness, creativity, art, and culture in adults. Thus, activities of this kind can be seen as extensions or developments of the transitional object. In the phenomenon of passionate love, lovers typically make use of love tokens, articles redolent of the beloved. Such objects can be viewed as something akin to Winnicott's transitional object.

In the past, a noble lady's "favour"—the personal article, such as the kerchief or girdle that she gave to her chosen knight, and other objects such as love letters, locks of hair, and so on—could be seen as forms of transitional object, but, in so far as these have a direct connection to the beloved, they are not transitional objects in the strict sense. Nowadays, our connection and communication with others depends to a great extent on technology. Virtual reality especially, with its real–unreal aspects, can take on qualities of transitional phenomena. In particular, in the field of relationships, I have found that the mobile phone can become a form of transitional object. One can see this happening for young people in the first flush of a love affair who cannot bear to be separated from their mobiles. Calling becomes a means of remembering and being remembered by the beloved. The mobile phone, like the landline phone, is a link, albeit a tenuous link, to an absent loved one. As such, telephones often appear in the dreams of analysands as an indirect but infinitely precious connection to the analyst. The phone can then signify love at a distance. However, it also seems to take on, by association, a particular significance in its own right. The mobile is carried around with one like a transitional object, looked at for reassurance and love, often almost caressed. It is also hated, thrown down in disgust, when it does not deliver what is hoped for. In short, it is treated here just like the baby's soft toy or comforter.

With the mobile phone, in particular, there is not only the possibility of the direct call or voicemail message, but also of the text. It is interesting to note that among lovers, especially the young, texting to each other is often the very first form of communication once mutual attraction has been recognized. Because texts can be sent at any time, night or day, they can also, alas, be missed or longed for at any time night or day. Unlike the beloved, but like the transitional object, the phone itself can be always within reach of the lover. Existing somewhere in the intermediary world between the object and the not-object, the mobile phone is both animate and inanimate, feelings most beautifully evoked by the poet Carol Ann Duffy in her poem "Text" (Duffy, 2005.) I quote it here in full:

Text

I tend the mobile now
like an injured bird.

We text, text, text
our significant words.

I re-read your first,
your second, your third,

look for your small *xx*,
feeling absurd.

The codes we send
arrive with a broken chord.

I try to picture your hands,
their image is blurred.

Nothing my thumbs press
will ever be heard.

In the opening verse, Duffy describes the quality of tenderness towards the object, which is described as if it were something alive. The sense of injury is transferred to the phone, neatly conveying the sense of an injury done either to the poet by the beloved, or to the beloved by poet. Is this injury, then, that of the object or the subject? Like the transitional object, it is "both me and not-me". In the next three verses, Duffy conveys the obsessive quality of attachment to the mobile phone because of its connection to the beloved. She then aptly conveys the ambivalence of the feelings about the beloved, transferred to the transitional object, with the "broken" chord of the text notification. The loss of the beloved is conveyed in the "blurred" image of the lover's hands that sent the message. As any lover knows, an object can be felt to be so intimately connected to the beloved as to evoke their physical presence, and yet, at the same time, it is not, and cannot ever be, the actual beloved. Thus, for the lover, the transitional object tantalizingly can, at the same time, evoke both a sense of the lover's presence and of their absence. It may even be that the very antisocial modern habit of texting one friend while sitting with another may derive from the significance of the mobile as a transitional object in its own right, much as the infant will hold on to its teddy or comforter *even while in the presence of its mother*.

The final lines of the poem beautifully evoke the ambivalence around the communication itself. Of course, no written text will ever be "heard" as such, but the choice of word and its emphasis by being placed at the beginning of the line-"Nothing my thumbs press / will ever be heard"—also suggests the idea (we could say the fear-fantasy) that the communication might never reach the beloved at all. In the same way, looking back in time to the baby's experience, the transitional object evokes the mother but is not the mother, and this provokes intensely ambivalent feelings: it gives something of the love object to the child, and yet, at the same time, denies her presence, since no transitional object is needed at the early stage during which she is felt to be an undifferentiated part of the infant.

There is yet another way in which the mobile phone can function as a transitional object: it enters into the transitional space between inner and outer worlds. The mobile phone, in a very practical way, can hide the secret of love away from the prying eyes of parents or spouses. For example, the ring can be heard and answered by the owner of the mobile without anyone else learning from whom the call is. The number of the sender or recipient of the calls or texts is not shown on the landline bills, and so the very fact of the communication with the lover can be kept hidden from the rest of the household. Last, and most intimate of all, if the phone is put on "silent" and set to vibrate, the lover can become the only one to be alerted to the call of the beloved and, furthermore, alerted in a way so secret and physical as to be erotic in itself.

It is also very interesting to note how the mobile phone can, conversely and just as readily, become the betrayer of love's secrets. Calls, unlike words, leave traces betraying the caller's identity, and that precious text, saved in the phone's memory, unlike memories stored only in the lover's mind, can be read by others. I have come across an extraordinary account of how a married man, out with his lover, accidentally hit one of the numbers in his mobile phone's contact list, thereby ringing his wife, who then, unnoticed by him at first, became privy to their conversation. Or another, when a married woman "accidentally" left the mobile phone bill visible, thereby betraying the multiple calls made to a single number, and thus revealing an affair. In such cases, of course, it could well be that part of the unconscious of the person wishes to reveal the truth, whether from guilt, a desire for transparency and honesty, or hostile feelings. In much the same way, a transitional object, such as a child's teddy bear, may both disguise *and* reveal the child's need for its mother.

We can see from this how Winnicott's contribution to understanding infants illuminates certain ordinary, healthy dynamics in the experience of falling in love.

Bowlby's contribution

Bowlby's important contribution to understanding relationships lies in his use of studies using direct observation of animal and child behaviour to understand infant development. From these, it could be predicted what might be the problems for a child, as it grows up, if its attachment behaviour was been not met with a suitable, attuned response. This approach is prospective, unlike that of psychoanalysis, which, in inducing the child's history from the account of the adult patient, is retrospective. I will return to

Bowlby's attachment theory as it relates to adult life in Chapter Three, but, in the context of exploring how the past shapes us, I would like to revisit his application of the notion of imprinting in the behaviour of animals.

Attraction as stemming from early imprinting

Bowlby describes how Lorenz, in his well-known experiments, showed that attachment behaviour can develop in ducklings and goslings without the young animals receiving any food or any other conventional reward (Bowlby, 1969). In the hours after they are hatched, the young tend to follow any moving object they see, whether that is "a mother bird, a man, a rubber balloon or a cardboard box". Having once followed a particular object, they come to prefer that object to others and, after a time, will follow no other. "The process of learning the characteristics of the object followed is known as imprinting" (*ibid.*, p. 259). Bowlby quotes experiments reviewed by J. P. Scott in 1963, showing that puppies can be induced to follow a man who not only gave them no reward at all, but who even punished them each time they attempted to follow "so that their only experience of human contact was painful" (*ibid.*, p. 261). After several weeks, the experimenter stopped the punishment, and the puppies not only ceased to run away from him, but spent even more time with him than the control puppies, whose approaches had been rewarded with uniform petting and kindness. These findings were confirmed in the case of lambs and monkeys. Even in animals, it would seem that mistreatment by care-givers can serve to increase the attachment behaviour in the young.

Relevant to our theme is Bowlby's own position: he first defines and then broadens out Lorenz's notion of imprinting. Thus, imprinting

> refers to whatever processes may be at work in leading the filial attachment behaviour of a young bird or mammal to become directed preferentially and stably towards one (or more) discriminated figure(s). By extension, it may also be used to refer to processes that lead other forms of behaviour to be directed preferentially towards objects, for example maternal behaviour towards particular young, and sexual behaviour towards particular mate(s). [*ibid.*, p. 210]

Thus, although pair bonding in adults is not the same as attachment between carers and children, there are aspects of the former that are a continuation of the latter. The idea of some kind of imprinting links the two.

The basis of attachment theory

Bowlby found that, in humans, there seems to be a sensitive period in the first year of life during which attachment behaviour develops most readily. This period probably starts not earlier than six weeks and ends by six months. After this, "stranger danger" responses are manifested. Due to this fact, forming an attachment to a new figure after this age becomes increasingly difficult. As with certain animals, "Once a child has become strongly attached to a particular figure, he tends to prefer that figure to all others, and such a preference tends to persist despite separation" (*ibid.*, p. 273.) Research showed that the variables which most clearly determined the type of figure to whom the children would become attached were the speed of the response to the child, and the intensity of the interaction with it (*ibid.*, p. 266).

Attachment behaviour would seem to have the evolutionary function of protection from predators. An isolated animal is much more susceptible to attack than one in a group. Attachment behaviour is elicited "particularly easily and intensely in animals which, by reason of age, size or condition, are especially vulnerable to predators, for example the young, pregnant females, the sick" (*ibid.*, pp. 276–267). We might also add those females that are actually carrying their young with them as they move. It is also always elicited at high intensity in situations of alarm, which are commonly situations when a predator is either sensed or suspected (*ibid.*, pp. 276–267). Furthermore, there is also a set of behaviours in the parent or parent substitute that is complementary to the attachment behaviour of the infant. These are care-giving behaviours. Bowlby describes how "signal behaviour", whereby a baby communicates to its mother in such a way that proximity is thereby increased, will elicit care-giving response. Signal behaviour can take different forms, such as crying, or gestures such as *raising the arms*, and of *trying to catch hold the mother's attention*. He notes that if the last is seen as an integral part of attachment behaviour, then it becomes more intelligible and can be looked upon more sympathetically.

> it is clearly vital that the mother of a child of under three or four years should know exactly where he is and what he is doing, and be ready to intervene should danger threaten; for him to keep advertising his whereabouts and activities to her and to continue doing so until she signals "message received" is therefore adaptive. [*ibid.*, p. 300]

Indeed, the complementary retrieving behaviour of a primate mother is that she "gathers the infant into her arms and holds him there" (*ibid.*, p. 292). In the wild, this keeps him or her safe from such dangers as predators, falling from a height, drowning, and so on. Vital behaviour indeed!

In general, behaviours common to a species have evolved to be of use in the stable environment in which the particular species would normally find itself. An environment is stable only as long as it remains within the range of that in which the species usually lives. Outside of these limits, the behaviour may become counterproductive and even destructive. Bowlby gives the example of how the behaviour of moths flying towards natural light becomes destructive for them in an artificial environment where the light is a naked flame.

Bowlby notes that although attachment behaviour and sexual behaviour are two distinct behavioural systems, they none the less have aspects in common and some, though not all, component patterns of each are shared. Herein lies a more specific explanation for Freud's discovery that later loves are later editions of the early love of the infant for its mother. Thus, in passionate love, much that seemed previously inexplicable becomes understandable. It seems likely that something akin to "imprinting", at least in its broader sense, is responsible for how individuals may experience an instinctual level of attraction (one that is not very amenable to reason) towards others who have certain traits of early attachment figures, most likely the mother in both sexes, and, to some extent, the father. These traits are likely to be not merely the more obvious ones of physical characteristics or of certain roles played, ones which are more likely to derive from the parent of the opposite sex, but, most crucially, those traits relating to the care-giver's (usually but not always the mother's) own style of parenting.

Clearly, if the attachment behaviour of the infant has not been met (often enough) with (sufficiently) reliable, intense, and attuned responses in the mother, then pathology ensues in the adult. Bowlby (1969, 1973, 1980) famously explored three phases of pre-dictable behaviour in all types of children separated from their mother after six months of age. In the first stage, *protest*, the child is acutely distressed, cries loudly, and might shake its cot or throw itself about. It looks and listens eagerly for its mother, and either rejects other carers or may cling desperately to a mother substitute. The child clearly expects the mother to return. In the second, *despair*, the active movements diminish or cease, the child cries monotonously or intermittently, and is withdrawn and inactive, making no demands on others. The child seems to be in mourning, and its behaviour suggests hopelessness. In the third stage, *detach-ment*, the child no longer rejects other substitutes, accepts care and food or toys, and may even smile and seem sociable. When the mother returns, the child does not show the normal attachment behaviour, but remains remote and apathetic and seems to have lost all interest in her. If the mother's absence is prolonged, it will, in time, act as if mothering and contact with humans has no signifi-cance; it commits less and less, and in time will stop attaching itself to anyone, becoming increasingly self-centred, occupying itself with material things rather than people. Such children seem cheer-ful and adaptive, but sociability is superficial and the child appears, to itself and to others, no longer to care for anyone.

This last is of tremendous significance: this independence, so often prized in our western society, is, here, a *lack*, a (pathological) inability to socialize. It represents a defence against what we might surmise to be the despair generated by unbearable loss or absence of the original primary carer. An entire society that overvalues inde-pendence, as does ours, may be revealing a collective pathology.

The child who has not been met with a sufficient amount of attuned responsiveness from the mother will, thus, as it grows to adulthood, continue to develop a pathological or insecure style of attachment. This style may manifest as either the over-clinging behaviour of a child who is uncertain of the reliability of its at-tachment figure, relating to the protest phase, or as "pathological detachment", where the child has cut off behaviours that have not resulted in a reassuring response from the care-giver, relating to Bowlby's third "detachment" phase. As he has described, the latter type then grows up to suppress its attachment needs and to convince itself and others that it does not need others.

It is not too difficult, then, to see how children with these two opposite forms of defensive behaviour can grow up to form either of two main insecure styles of relationship. Behind the symptoms that Klein noted in the "flight from loneliness" is Bowlby's idea of the insecure style of relating that came later to be known as "anxious" or "preoccupied". Behind Klein's "flight from dependency" is Bowlby's idea of the style of relating that came later to be known as "avoidant". It is very common to see two people, one with an anxiously attached style of relating and the other with an avoidantly attached style, becoming attracted to one another. This often results in a kind of "push-me-pull-you" form of "dance". Pickering (2008) gives a thorough analysis of the details of these "relational configurations".

We must note that Bowlby (1969) claims that "no form of behaviour is accompanied by stronger feeling than is attachment behaviour" (*ibid.*, p. 257). He also describes how studies in the Ganda and Scotland show that, contrary to possible expectations,

> the infant who begins by showing an intense attachment to a principle figure is reported as significantly more likely to direct his social behaviour to other discriminated figures as well, whereas an infant who is weakly attached is more likely to confine all his social behaviour to a single figure. [*ibid.*, p. 367]

It would seem that "the more insecure a child's attachment to his principal figure is the more inhibited it is likely to be in developing attachments to other figures" (*ibid.*, p. 368).

Hence, if mate selection and falling in love share patterns in common with the early infant's relationship to its mother, as Bowlby asserts, then negative patterns of behaviour will be carried over into adult love relationships. It would seem that in ordinary friendship (where liking rather than passionate love predominates) there is more possibility of conscious reasoning, present feeling responses, and mature learning influencing behaviour. For example, friends who are overly unresponsive may be more readily dropped and those who are responsive more readily sought out. However, in falling in love (where sexual passion predominates), behaviour will be less amenable to reason, to the feedback from present feelings, and to mature learning. Conditioning is more likely to prevail and the effects of "imprinting" will be at their height. Where there is no, or little, negative imprinting, this will not be too much of a problem, but where early attachment learnings have been negative, then they will adversely affect later relationships.

In therapy, patient and detailed work is needed to explore the style of a person's relating and to uncover those early imprinted patterns from infancy. One woman was caught in a pattern of relationships with emotionally abusive men. She herself, when young, had been used as a parent figure by her own mother and had not been seen as a child in her own right. Release of the painful, angry, despairing, and anxious feelings clustered around insecure attachment behaviour can help to unhook instinctual attraction from negative conditioning, and, more specifically, the selection of a mate does not have to be synonymous with such things as unbearable pain, abuse, invasion, rejection, abandonment, or uncertainty.

Again, in order to achieve this, what is needed is a painstakingly detailed exploration of the minutiae of the patient's relationship behaviour, past and present, including how they interpret the words and actions of their partner, how they then respond to them, what effects their responses may have, and so on. The more behavioural way of working needs to go hand in hand with the work of uncovering early childhood patterns and is also crucial, otherwise the insights deriving from analysis will remain theoretical and be of no practical value.

The limitations of Winnicott's and Bowlby's theories

More recently, there has been greater recognition of the importance of the role played by the father, even in those early months (for example, Samuels [1985]), and the early influence of siblings or their lack. This had previously been much neglected in psychoanalytic discourse. Further, especially if we look beyond specifically Western, industrialized cultures, we need to acknowledge the influences of the extended family and of communities in even the very early life of the infant. A grandparent, aunt or uncle, an older sibling, a step-parent, or second wife or husband of a child's father or mother, a nanny, or even a maid or servant may have been more of a primary carer to that child than either of its biological parents. Indeed, a British Nigerian woman, mother of a close friend of my son, told me incidentally, "In Nigeria, the children belong to the whole community." A Glaswegian friend has memories of days when neighbours would actively look out for the children of family, friends, or neighbours, acting as substitute parents when these were not around. We must also recognize the limitations to comparisons between animal and human behaviour and be aware of the fact that adult styles of attachment develop in more sophisticated ways than seen in infant attachment behaviour. Some of these have been elaborated more recently, and there are now many more finely tuned descriptions of the different styles of attachment.

Since pathological styles of attachment can thoroughly undermine love relationships, I shall outline a way of categorizing them, drawing on and developing Pickering's categories in her book *Being in Love* (Pickering, 2008). In Chapter Eight, Pickering, drawing on Holmes' work, elaborates on Bowlby's original secure, insecure (clinging), and insecure (self reliant) categories. The last two are known as preoccupied–ambivalent and dismissing–avoidant, respectively. Insecure–ambivalent individuals fear and expect abandonment and cling to the love object, terrified of separation. Insecure–avoidant individuals fear and expect intrusion and shy away from closeness, fearing or dismissing it. Pickering describes the various relational dynamics based on pair combinations of each of the different styles: secure with secure, secure with insecure (either preoccupied or avoidant); preoccupied–ambivalent with dismissive–avoidant, avoidant with avoidant, and, last, preoccupied–ambivalent with preoccupied–ambivalent. Pickering's description of the typical dynamics of each of these configurations is very thorough, and clinically of value not only for couple work, but also in therapeutic work with a person in a couple relationship.

In Chapter Ten, she describes what she calls "Narcissus–Echo relationships", where the latter partner is the admirer and the former is the admired. Again, she explores the dynamics between Narcissus–Echo, Narcissus–Narcissus, and Echo–Echo type pairings.

I suggest that it would be useful to divide insecure relational dynamics into two further categories and discriminate between those that are based on *fear* of closeness or separation (issues of dependence–independence) and those that are based on *low self esteem* (issues of inner fullness or depletion).

Let us look at the clingingly attached–avoidantly attached pairings that are based on fear. In this dynamic, as Pickering points out, perfectly valid needs for distance or closeness in a relationship are experienced as a polarity by each partner: that is, as an "either/or" rather than a "both/and". One partner (clingingly attached) projects the inner abandoning early attachment figure outwards on to the other and fears abandonment from them, while the other partner (distantly attached) projects an inner intruding early figure on to the other and fears invasion or engulfment by them. The clingingly attached partner identifies with dependence, but has repressed his/her own autonomy and independence needs, while the distantly attached partner has done the reverse.

The second set of insecure relational dynamics relates to adoring–adored dynamics based on low self esteem. We could describe this as a "richness–impoverishment" dynamic. In the adored–adoring form of pairing, one partner (adoringly attached) projects their inner richness on to the other and seeks value by attaching themselves to a valued other, while the other partner (dismissively attached) projects their inner emptiness on to the other and seeks value from that other's adoration. The adoringly attached partner identifies with a sense of inferiority and has repressed his/her own sense of superiority, and the dismissively attached person has done the reverse. We can see how the pathologies of sado-masochism and narcissism overlap with these insecure attachment styles.

I think it is helpful to see the (a) clingingly and (b) adoringly attached styles as two distinct categories within Bowlby's "anxiously attached" styles and the (c) distantly and (d) dismissively attached styles as two distinct categories within his "avoidantly attached" styles. Further, (a) and (c) (the clinging and distant styles) together form a combination pertaining to the nearness–separation polarity, while (b) and (d) (the adoring and dismissive styles) form another combination pertaining to a richness–impoverishment dynamic. These elaborations on Bowlby's original categories give us ones that are more sophisticated and more nuanced, thereby providing us with more useful tools in working with relational dynamics.

Jung's contribution

Jung's theories lay quite a lot of stress on the historical experience of a child, although he did not flesh this out much at all. He also describes how a person's relationship to the opposite sex is based to a large degree, especially early on in life, on internalized experiences of the mother and other actual women in one's life in the case of the man, or the father and all experiences of other actual men in one's life in the case of the woman. These ideas are mostly explored in terms of individuation, so I shall explore them later (Chapter Four).

There remain two themes that I would like to explore in a bit more detail, as I think that those relational psychologies that acknowledge the basic healthy social needs of the infant (the "human givens", if you will) have contributed explanations that help to make greater sense of them.

Sado-masochism and Benjamin's contribution

Benjamin, writing from a relational psychology perspective, revisits Freud's ideas on sadism and masochism (Benjamin, 2008.) She sees sado-masochistic pathology rather as arising from disturbances of the ordinary need to receive recognition from, and accord recognition to, the other. For relationships to function, we are required to see the other as a person in their own right, as a self who is the centre of their own world in the same way as we ourselves are the centre of ours. A failure of a proper development of this symmetry in the mother–child relationship can result in sado-masochistic defences. Masochism will be to the fore when the child has been made to adapt too much to the mother, and sadism when the mother has adapted too much to the child. I will return to her book in Chapter Three, to explore how she relates these to gender issues.

While her insights are extremely valuable, I find that I do not agree with her symmetrical version of the aetiology of sadism and masochism. It would, indeed, seem to be true that a masochistic defence *can* be set up by the lack of adaptation of the mother or carer(s) of the infant, but I do not find in practice that it is necessarily so, or that sadism is necessarily set up by the opposite problem: that of the carer or mother who is overly adaptive to her infant at the expense of herself. Benjamin is quite right to advert to the problems, more relevant as the child grows older, set up by an overly-adaptive mother, and these have been too little emphasized by Winnicott and others. Indeed, one can see that over the generations, the various theories have one way or another tended to reveal a pendulum swing between these two opposing modalities: adaptation of the mother to the child and adaptation of the child to the mother.

The overly adaptive parent does not, I would maintain, *necessarily* set up a sadistic defence in the child. What I think is created in this case is self-centred, egotistic behaviour in an individual who has, thus, been taught that the whole world revolves around him or her and who has not learnt well enough how to adapt to others. The child, of course, does not feel loved in being thus indulged, since, as Melanie Klein notes, the mother in this case is really fulfilling not her child's needs, but her own unfulfilled needs from *her* childhood (Klein, 1937.) Such a love in the mother is, thus, narcissistic. The "spoiled" child, now grown into adulthood, feels a more or less conscious guilt at "having it all their own way" and will, again consciously or unconsciously, resent this. Even as they tyrannize those they love, they will, deep down, hope against hope that someone will love them enough to challenge them. Indeed, if they are lucky enough to find a partner who is able and willing to do this, then they may find themselves able to change. If they cannot, they may simply leave the challenger to find a new partner who, like their mother, will be overly adaptive to their needs. Often, they will have selected a partner who will merely play Echo to their Narcissus. Sometimes, in the boredom a Narcissus feels with such an arrangement, one can see the stirrings of the desire to be confronted. One sees overly adaptive women thunderstruck by a husband who has walked out on them, failing to see the part they inadvertently played. "But how could he leave? I gave him so much," they ask in bewilderment, not realizing that the very attitude of letting him have it all his own way might have been at least a factor in his leaving.

I would suggest, rather, that extremes of sadism and masochism come from the same roots: both are last-ditch mechanisms to protect survival when a person feels completely helpless in relation to the onslaught of intolerable pain. This last-ditch, archetypal defence of the core self is movingly described in Kalsched (1996). As I see it, it is the traumatic nature of the suffering of the child (and this trauma can include the ongoing daily trauma of such events as neglect) that polarizes the psyche in this way, much as the violent electrical discharge of a thunderstorm polarizes the air into positive and negative ions.

We know from contemporary political history that if a child (or an adult, for that matter) experiences an extreme of physical or emotional torture, the internal dynamics of torturer–tortured are deposited. Child soldiers are created by forcing them into acts of brutality, such as slaughtering their own parents or peers. Torturers are trained by having them first be tortured. I am not, of course, saying that the mother or father will have set out to torture her or his child (although, of course, all therapists must keep in mind that there are rare cases of exactly this kind of acting out behaviour in a very disturbed mother, for example, Schreiber's description [Schreiber, 1973] of the story of "Sybil" and her eleven-year analysis), but the parent's own pathology might create an experience torture in the child.

I would suggest, then, that a person in these circumstances is likely to react with *either* of the two poles of the one defence and produce either a masochistic or a sadistic pattern of behaviour. What I think masochism does is to say, "If I submit, maybe I will survive". We can compare this choice to that of an animal under threat who exhibits submissive behaviour in order not to be attacked. We saw how, in the case of a moth flying into a flame, Bowlby gives an example of how a species' adaptation to ordinary environments can become destructive in extraordinary ones. In a human, this will mean exhibiting whatever behaviour seems to be required of them. If the mother wants docile, her baby will "do" docile, if good, good, if nurturing, nurturing, and so on. I can remember a poignant televised documentary where a young boy misbehaved every time he sensed that his parents might be about to erupt into an argument that might, as it had done so often, turn violent. Even though he got punished for his behaviour, it clearly served the purpose of distracting his parents from their row, a possibility that the boy must have felt to be more terrifying than whatever violence they might mete out to him. A very good expression of this almost unconditional readiness to adapt to the other is given in the film *Tootsie*. At the beginning of the story, the hero, Michael Dorsey, an out-of-work actor who has an appalling reputation for being difficult, has become so desperate to get work that he is ready to be whatever is required of him (Schisgal & Gelbart, 1982.) At an audition, he clearly is not fitting the bill. He asks the director if his reading was not right.

"No, the reading was fine. You're just the wrong height."

"Oh, I can be taller."

"No, no, you don't understand—we're looking for somebody shorter."

"Oh, look! I don't have to be this tall. See! I'm wearing lifts—I can be shorter."

"I know, but—really we're looking for somebody different."

"I can be different."

It is this theme of having permanently to be *different*—anything but what one actually is—that reveals the poignancy of this kind of false self presentation.

Conversely, the sadistic response can also contain something more like: "You must see—I will *make* you see—what it is like when you hurt me this much". I think the person could be trying to teach the other what it is like to be on the receiving end of the helplessness. Perhaps sadism, in that case, expresses more hope; hope in the other being able to respond appropriately. Bowlby describes this endeavour in his stage of protest in the abandoned baby. Anger shows that things are still hopeful. The child, at this point, still believes that its mother is capable of response and can be taught by the child's anger not ever to subject the baby to that degree of distress again. Anger has a pedagogic value.

But both of these constellations, sadism and masochism, I would suggest, are, therefore, two sides of a reaction to complete helplessness in the face of intolerable pain or threat of disintegration when survival itself is felt to be directly at stake. Any infant is, to a great extent, actually helpless in relation to an adult carer, and survival issues can be so readily constellated. Later, the child grown adult, and now in possession of a more developed ego, has a whole possible repertoire of choices in relation to feeling cornered but, since they will probably have learnt only one or two basic styles of defence, will feel and think that there is only one way to go about this. So, a self-destructive pattern of sadism or masochism, having been set up in the first place, is then maintained.

The one thing that both the sadist and the masochist cannot bear is the experience of helplessness in relation to intense pain that can be re-evoked. I think that the elaborately worked out sado-masochistic erotic scenarios can sometimes be an attempt to replay the terrible script, only now with a new element to replace the old helplessness. Both the sadist and the masochist can now feel in control. The sado-masochistic "arrangement" offers each of the actors the illusion of *choosing* the pain, helplessness, or submission of the self or the other, when, in the original formative scenario, it was not chosen at all, but inflicted. But, alas, the fact that this feel-good ending does not convince is demonstrated by the need for endless repetitions of the same rituals. On the other hand, if the individual can begin to tolerate the experience of helplessness in relation to almost unbearable pain, then the pattern could be trans-formed.

However, sado-masochism, acted out in this way, is towards the extreme end of survival mechanisms. What one might think of as "normal" masochism or "normal" sadism occurs, as we have seen, when perhaps the trauma is not "off the scale": healthy sadism, when the lover, whose attachment figure is absent or is not enough attuned to them, has the reasonable hope that their passionate protest might teach the beloved never to do that again, or healthy masochism, that their adaptive behaviour might placate an angry beloved. This give and take, the negotiations involved between self and other, are the stuff of ordinary intimate relationships. The more extreme response may be seen in infancy, when the feelings are more primitive and intense, in intensely passionate love, when primitive emotions may be more readily evoked, and in extremes of pathology. The last two, intensely passionate love and relation-ship pathology, may, of course, occur together and be all the more difficult for that.

Freud saw women as *inherently* masochistically orientated, and that the girl's proper resolution of the Oedipal complex was, effectively, to submit, to accept passive aims. Benjamin's work challenges gendered assumptions such as these (Benjamin, 2008). In my reading of sado-masochism, we can use Bowlby's notion of adaptation to one's environment to see that, in a survival situation, whether or not one placates an aggressor or confronts them depends on *one's best assessment, accurate or inaccurate, of one's likelihood of success with either strategy*. A truly powerless group, whether that is Victorian womanhood, black slaves, or prison camp inmates, will tend to adopt placating strategies. Yet, to the extent to which they become stronger after empowerment, they become more able to use aggression to repel the threat. The paradox is that once a person becomes confident that they have the real possibility of protecting their autonomy, they have less need of any display of aggression. Secure assertion often suffices.

Bliss revisited

We can explore one final possible explanation as to why falling in love can provoke such powerful emotions. We looked earlier at the particular quality of the satiation of a baby at its mother's breast when well fed and, as we are now more aware, how fulfilment of the need for bonding (closeness of skin contact, eye contact, smell, tone of voice, etc.) enhances the experience. Freud often uses the terms "pleasure" and "unpleasure"; he sees, to my mind rightly, these two as a pair of opposites which drive a great deal of conscious and unconscious behaviour. The seeking of pleasure and the avoidance of pain are two motivations that characterize all animals (perhaps, in some form, all living things). However, it is interesting to note that our language gives us other words, too, which connote different qualities of pleasant experience: we do not have the term "pleasure" alone for goods we might seek, but also happiness, joy, and so on. Pleasure might be understood as the more basic (i.e., animal or mammalian) aim, happiness as a more human, more evolved one; such things as joy or fulfilment may be even more so. Yet, we also have another term on this pleasure spectrum, and that is "bliss". Bliss would seem to have a different quality altogether, one that seems to cut across the distinction between more primitive needs and more evolved ones. Freud himself (Freud, 1905d) writes of early feeding,

> No-one who has seen a baby sinking back satiated from the breast and falling asleep with flushed cheeks and a blissful smile can escape the reflection that this picture persists as a prototype of the expression of sexual satisfaction in later life. [*ibid.*, p. 322]

Freud, here, is describing, in the satiated baby, a state of bliss, and he notes the connection between the state of bliss in infancy and that later state after a satisfactory love-making. Yet, wherein exactly does this connection lie? Clearly, the adult human being, with their highly developed ego, a developed capacity for complex feelings, for developed imagination, refined sense perception, and so on, is, in their love-making, experiencing far more than the bliss of a suckling baby, for all the intimate connection between these two states. Yet, I would go so far as to suggest that it is a state of bliss above all, in one form or another, for which the adult lover longs. We saw earlier how Klein (1957) makes a version of this claim: the infant's bliss experienced in being suckled is

> not only the basis of sexual gratification (Freud) but of all later happiness and makes possible the feeling of unity with another person; such unity means being fully understood, which is essential for every happy love relation or friendship. [*ibid.*, p. 188]

Conversely, I would suggest that a loss of this state of bliss, especially a sudden severance from this feeling of unity, can cause a reaction in the psyche that can have an almost psychotic nature, certainly a borderline quality to it. It is very interesting to note that in the borderline personality disorder literature (the European title of "emotionally unstable" is a more accurate description than "borderline") (BPD World, 2007), symptoms are described which any therapist might well recognize as a description, albeit extreme, of a client who has fallen in love. It is addressed to the person suffering from BPD:

> You can alternate between being flooded with emotion and being numb to all feeling. Whatever feeling state predominates at the moment seems to last forever. Emotional pain then seems endless

and excruciating. You are unable to tap past experience and to appreciate that pain is only temporary and can be survived.

When applied to relationships this particular disturbance of memory means that the last encounter colours the whole relationship—if parted on an angry note you may wish for revenge. If parted on pleasing time [the relationship is] idealized and [you may] desperately long for a reunion. This intensely black and white quality of feelings can turn disappointment to rage. Rage may be turned against the self . . . When you lose a relationship, you lose the inner sense of goodness that accompanied it. Since abandonment brings with it feelings of emptiness, it is avoided at all costs.

However, even in those who by no means could be given the label of BPD, I would suggest that the situation of falling in love can precipitate a very similar a crisis with almost identical symptoms, at least within the prescribed context of the love affair. Sometimes, this crisis has been termed an encapsulated psychosis, but, unless there is otherwise considerable pathology, I prefer to think of it as a "psychotic *part*" of an individual. It is a part often represented by a mad figure in a patient's dream, or of a disturbed patient in the dreams of a psychotherapist. We will take up this image again in Chapter Four.

Yet, we can also see that symptoms described in the BDP Newsletter could apply not only to a borderline state of psychosis, or even an encapsulated psychosis, or a psychotic part, but also to the state of infancy. The intensity of the feeling, its rapid alternation between almost overwhelming emotion and then numbness, the lack of laid down memories that can inform you that this emotion is not going to last forever, the absence of an awareness that you can survive this pain, the desire to punish the loved one, the idealization and the splitting and very black and white quality to the feelings, the way in which disappointment turns to rage, and so on, all these have been expertly described by Melanie Klein in so much of her writing on infancy.

Falling in love is both entrancing and terrifying because of the possibility it holds for transporting us back to childhood and whatever there lies unfinished. The fact that we might "fall into" very early baby experiences, not yet fully worked through, helps to explain the quality of the experience. However, I would suggest it is, in part, precisely because of its ability to provoke a state of bliss that gives it this power. This theme of bliss is very rich and there is more to be said on the subject. I shall return to it later in Chapters Three and Five.

Two detailed profiles

Let us digress a little: I would like to flesh out my theme by imagining what it is like for someone who has not been "held" as a child: that is, not been given a sufficient regular experience of a mother's attuned attention and care. I will draw on the accounts of many clients to give a composite picture.

This kind of lack is trauma, indeed, but not as we know it. It is not the trauma of a one-off event, or even of a particular series of events that could be counted. It is the trauma of a whole way of life. A child has grown up without a sense of being the significant other in the eyes of the person who is the child's own significant other. If the parents, and especially the mother in those early months, are not able to give the child that experience, then the child will not feel loved where it loves, nor wanted where it wants. As I mentioned earlier, the child will feel unloved by *that which is the very source of love itself*, as far as the child can experience it at the time. At that tender age, it cannot fault its parents; they are like gods in relation to the child (see Chapter Four), so it must assume itself to be unlovable. The child yearns, but knows not what it yearns for. It feels a lack, yet cannot pin-point any distinct thing lacking, and so assumes this lack to be some inherent characteristic of its own self. There are two main reasons why it is so hard for the child to pin-point what is lacking: one is, of course, that it cannot know what it lacks since it will not have had any experience of what it is missing, and second, because that lack forms the very medium in which the child moves and has its being, it can no more discern that lack than a fish could know that it swims in water!

The whole of that person's life, then, is coloured by the "fact" of their being unlovable. This "fact" will have been pushed down into the unconscious as too unbearable to realize, and so will have become all the more powerful for not being conscious. Yet, all later love relationships will bear this stamp, and the child, now an adult, is likely to be attracted to those who in some way duplicate this experience and thereby confirm this "fact". And the trauma will not be confined to the area of love relationships, but the child grown adult will live in a world in which it is fundamentally unloveable, in which the very sustaining force that makes life sweet is missing. In this world, life is only harsh, ungrateful, and fundamentally a struggle; to be is to be exhausted, and the person survives rather than lives; being loved where one loves, loving where one is loved, is an impossible dream, and death itself seems to be the only release. Even if they are not consciously suicidal in any way, those who live in this "reality" suffer from a deep death wish. Death as cessation of awareness, or perhaps death as containing some kind of promise of a happier afterlife, seems to offer the only possible chance of respite from this deep, deep pain.

When we start to look at adult passionate love relationships as a replaying of old scripts, scripts authored not only by ourselves, but also by our environment, especially those to do with the first "love affair" with the mother, many things can begin to make sense. We can see more clearly why falling in love can be fraught with danger; the old pains that could be evoked, will be felt to be unbearable. If a person with such a past can bear to allow themselves to fall in love, then it is likely that all hell will be let lose.

The *anxiously attached* lover will feel that their very survival depends on the beloved's attention and regard and valuation, just as it did, in fact, so depend on those same qualities in the mother. Desperate to experience at last what they have never known, that is, what it is to be special to someone, they will hope against hope that this one time will prove all of their earlier life wrong. They are likely to try to do anything to prevent this chance from failing and, therefore, having to "admit" to themselves, as it seems to them, once and for all, that they really are unlovable. If here, too, the lover lets them down, or appears to let them down, this will be unbearable. One woman described the experience of waiting every night for a phone call from a neglectful boyfriend as being like that of having a rib taken out each and every night. For her, it was an experience of torture almost impossible to imagine. And, of course, it can be the very intensity of the desperation itself that may undermine the relationship. Yearning as they are to be loved, a person with such a history may adapt too much, they will cling on too hard to a poor relationship long after others, able to be more philosophical about it, would have said, "I guess he or she just doesn't fancy me in the way I fancy them". Or they might drive a potentially suitable lover away by an intensity that can alarm the candidate. In my opinion, it is these sorts of case that require an analysis or psychotherapy that is prepared to carry and work though the intense transferences that will be elicited.

The *avoidantly attached* lover would have learnt that intimacy comes at far too great a price. It might be, for example, that the child learnt that attachment demanded an abrogation of autonomy. The child might have been used as an extension of the parent's own narcissistic needs. The "gods" then seem continually to demand sacrifice or intrude in human affairs and make life dangerous. There is the same yearning for something the child cannot know exists, but intimacy equates with invasion, and others must be kept at bay to prevent that happening. It may then be the case, as the child grows into adulthood, that their very aloofness will threaten any new relationship. A person with such an attachment style will hide the depths of their need for the other, sometimes even from themselves. They will come across as cold, when deep down they might well feel the opposite. As soon as they get the slightest whiff of intrusion (and that might even be projected rather than real), they will act as if indifferent and perhaps become distant or cut off from the relationship. Sometimes, the aloofness is a defence against a hidden fear of abandonment. Either way, the individual will provoke their partner into becoming more demanding by their very aloofness. Even as they try to change the behaviour, they might find that such defences just kick in without their being able to do anything about it. Again, such an intransigent pattern may well need in-depth transference work to change the complex.

What the relational psychologies add

In general, the relational psychologies, with their insights into healthy, functioning relationships, give us further and more detailed evidence as to why falling in love can have so much power for us. Infant studies, which have uncovered the rich social life of the baby and how it learns the relational skills needed for the future, show us especially what can go wrong when these needs are

not met. Attachment difficulties from childhood will affect all relationships in adulthood, and, therefore, intimate relationships also.
The dangers that beset passionate love relationship so often arise
from these early difficulties and, as we have seen from the profiles
above, can undermine again and again either the possibilities of
falling in love in the first place, or of the love maturing in such a
way that it has a chance of it being reciprocated.

But when we have explored all there is to explore and taken into
account all we can of both the inner and outer worlds of childhood,
have we said all there is to say about falling in love? It must, of
course, be admitted that we have not: human beings do not only
relate to others as babies and children, but are members of a social
species and have needs for others in ways that are specific to adulthood. There is, for example, the whole area of adult life to do with
the finding of a suitable mate and the having and bringing up of
young. There is more, then, that needs to be said.

PART I

(B) What we are: embodied beings

CHAPTER THREE

The scientific discourse

W e have explored narratives that help us understand why passionate love can provoke so many intense negative feelings and can reveal an underlying pathology that has its roots in childhood. Yet, we must ask ourselves why, then, do we fall in love? Why is passionate love so prevalent? Indeed, despite what may be thought to be the case, both anthropological and historical studies would seem to suggest that passionate love is and always has been an important, if not major, mode of pairing in society. More recent historical and anthropological research has corrected a bias that had deemed it to be exceptional. Further understanding is afforded us by the natural sciences, and especially by the emerging neurosciences. We shall, therefore, go on to explore what emerges from research in these various fields.

The contribution of social history

Careful study of primary sources, such as parish records, an understanding of the statistics, the context in which they are applied, and a greater interest in social history can provide us with a broader and more accurate picture of betrothal and marriage customs than previously. The social historian Pounds (1994) maintains that in traditional societies in Britain, for example, from the Iron Age to the industrial revolution, most marriages "arose from the mutual attraction of the two people". The arranged marriage was more an affair of those with land or property to be divided. Due mainly to economic necessity, couples married much later than is generally supposed, a woman at around her early to mid twenties and a man at around 25–30. Therefore, in practice, it was betrothal that was the most important step in a marriage. Although couples did not live together after betrothal, again out of financial necessity, 'at the popular level pre-nuptial intercourse was taken for granted'. Despite what the Church said, in practice, fertility was often tested out in this way before a marriage and, extrapolating from church records, we can deduce that many brides were pregnant at the time of their marriage. It is easy to see how the vast majority of people, agricultural workers without property, would seldom have much objection to their young people marrying as they fancied, and even in those instances where marriages were "arranged" by brokers or the families, this could be more a case of settling financial affairs between a man and a woman who had already chosen one another.

We have a biased understanding of what is then termed "romantic love", based on the influence of literary sources which were and still are more likely to explore the obstacles to love, such as in extramarital affairs, as these make for a good story! This has led us to assume that passionate love was far from the norm. A marginalization of passionate love, seen as "romantic" love, has thus ensued, which has, in turn, led to its denigration. Contemporary findings from social history can help to correct this distortion.

The contribution of ethology and anthropology

In the field of depth psychology, although Freud speculated about traditional societies, it was Bowlby, and others such as Ainsworth and Jung, who conducted their own direct anthropological studies or drew on those studies available at the time. Drawing on parallels with primates and other mammals, Bowlby (1969) stresses repeatedly that attachment behaviour in adults cannot be seen simply as immature. For this reason, he eschews Freud's term "dependency", which is still in use. Rather, *adult* attachment behaviour is:

> a straightforward continuation of attachment behaviour in childhood . . . In sickness and in calamity, adults often become demanding of others; in conditions of sudden danger or disaster a person will almost certainly seek proximity to another known and trusted person. In such circumstances an increase of attachment behaviour is recognized by all as natural. To dub attachment behaviour in adult life regressive is indeed to overlook the vital role that it plays in the life of man from the cradle to the grave. [*ibid.*, pp. 255–256]

To illustrate this with a post-industrial example, we can take a very common work environment: the office. In this quintessentially adult environment, individuals are likely to form particular relationships to one or two, perhaps more, attachment figures. In a crisis, those bonds will serve a very useful function. Let us suppose a fire breaks out in the building: the fire alarm is sounded, and everyone follows the usual drill and gathers outside the building. If an individual has a particular friend who is "rooting" for them, it is they who will bear that person in mind and it will be they who will most likely to notice if that particular acquaintance is absent. If everyone in the building has formed at least one or two such attachments, it is not hard to see how a group as a whole may stand a better chance of being saved. To be in any situation where no such attachment figures are present is to be in a situation of increased danger and, thus, to be made more anxious. A person who, for whatever reason, has no one who is "rooting" for them in any situation and who must then fend for themselves will quite naturally find life more stressful and more anxious-making. This is the case even for fit and able, fully-functioning adults throughout their remaining lives. The ordinary exigencies of life, for example, conditions such as a particular dangerous crisis, illness, pregnancy, the rearing of young, old age, and dying, all exacerbate this need. The desire for the companionate love from a significant other can be seen as a particular case of this more general need.

The contribution of gender studies

Throughout the history of depth psychology, many theorists have ventured to make statements about sex differences and gender differences based on notions taken from social anthropology. These notions, or the anthropological studies from which they derive, vary from the frankly primitive to the more sophisticated, but they all have a bearing on our understanding of the phenomenon of passionate love. To the extent to which they are not based on detailed anthropological research, they are more like myths: myths of a gendered polarity.

For Freud, "masculinity" and "femininity" are essentially characterized by the active–passive polarity. For Jung, the polarity of gender is that of Logos–Eros. At first, Jung thought that actual women and actual men reflected this directly, and that men were thinking types and women feeling types (Jung, 1971). He later abandoned this classification when he found both types represented in men and women. Winnicott (1971) also had the idea of the "pure male and pure female elements", whether in males or females. For him, this pure male–female polarity is essentially the "doing–being" polarity. Post Jungians, such as Erich Neumann, talk of matriarchal consciousness as an all pervading, conceiving, and fructifying consciousness, and patriarchal consciousness as compartmentalized, and Claremont de Castillejo (1973), elaborating on Neumann, sees the masculine as to do with focused thinking and the feminine with diffuse thinking.

What is very important to note here is that each of these serious and well-respected practitioner–thinkers has given an *entirely different* definition of what are the essential masculine and feminine characteristics in human beings! Note, also, how the definition of what is the pure male and what is the pure female element changes over time. Note again how it is nearly always held, at least according to the values of the time, that whatever characteristics are defined as male are seen as more developed or superior versions of those characteristics that are defined as female. Thus, it becomes clear, with gender being such a moveable feast, that these polarities, as such, are not simply "human givens" as has been supposed. Today, in the popular *Men Are from Mars, Women Are from Venus* (Gray, 2002), we have a new version, with men as the fixers and women as the talkers. Yet, in certain societies, we come across women involved in hard physical labour while their menfolk discuss the state of affairs over a drink!

Hillman (1972) has given an extremely insightful analysis of the role of fantasy in gender definitions; he cites a great number of examples of arguments of one kind or another for the inferiority of women in the classical and patristic traditions. For example, in theories of reproduction, he notes, "wherever it was conceded that there was female seed, or where the even rarer concession was made that such seed was necessary for reproduction, female seed was inferior" (p. 226). One very cogent detail in particular that he cites is the example of the supposed shape of the egg of male and female chicks. Although all the eggs are roughly ovoid, a variation of shape as to more or less ovoid or spherical was noticed. Aristotle held that the male chick develops from the sharp-pointed, more ovoid shaped egg. Hillman notes that for Aristotle, "That egg which is most true to the nature of eggness . . . most perfected and actualized as egg, naturally produces the male chick" (p. 234). He goes on to say that the philosopher Albertus Magnus, writing centuries later, contradicts Aristotle's opinion and claims that the more spheroid eggs contain the male chick embryos. This is because the sphere is the most perfect of figures in solid geometry. Hillman gives further examples and concludes, "Whichever side one held to—long or round—the female was always proved inferior. Even the egg, the female symbol par excellence, had superior and inferior aspects, and could be used to adduce female inferiority" (1972, p. 235).

All the foregoing are gender stereotypes: ideas about what men and women are *inherently*. Such stereotypes, if generally accurate, can sometimes be useful, but are nearly always dangerous. They can also be inaccurate. Who, we must ask, for example, is it who is making these claims? Are they unbiased? More specifically, stereotypes, when applied by one person as subject to another as object, will always involve the operation of fantasy: a projection of certain elements within the subject on to the object.

Feminist writers have done much to deconstruct notions of gender, arguing that, while a person's sex is a biological given, their gender can be viewed as a construct that is inevitably based on the sociological, political, and economic context in which they find themselves. This context varies from place to place and age to age. These writers have made cogent criticisms of theories of femininity and masculinity based on a variety of reasons, not least due to the recognition of how a previously patriarchal bias influences the thinking in even the most subtle of ways. de Beauvoir's *The Second Sex* (1949), while needing modification, remains a classic exploration of how our language, our attitudes, our whole way of thinking, is predicated on the assumption that the male is the paradigmatic version of the human being and the female is a derivative of this.

More specifically related to our field are the works of other, contemporary feminists who have sought to explode the fantasies of romantic love as an important mind-set whereby women can remain trapped in a form of bondage to the men they love. Benjamin (1988), for example, uses the philosophy of dialectic materialism to analyse how men and women can fall into master–slave relationships, and how this polarization is a flight from the difficulties of a negotiated relationship of mutual adaptedness to the other.

Of other feminist writers who treat falling in love as their theme, Evans (2003), Sullivan (1999), and Langford (1999) show very good examples of how "romantic love" can be a dangerous trap for women especially. Any woman who finds herself in love would do well to read these works as a kind of inoculation against such a dangerous infection. Greer (1970) fruitfully compares the psychological effects of slavery on Black Americans with those of oppression on women. She notes that there were some slaves who preferred to stay in servitude rather than take the liberty that the American Civil War had won for them. Destructive conditioning, what is termed internalized racism or sexism, cannot be changed overnight!

These works raise some very interesting questions. If notions of "romantic love" can cause undue expectations, should such idea be jettisoned? It is indeed true, as many of the writers above point out, that the notion of "romantic love" derives from a particular discourse within the Western tradition and, as such, arrives in the life of an individual already impregnated with many layers of meaning. Yet, "passionate love", flourishing both within and without social constraints, has always evoked a great deal of interest, and has been extolled, or deplored, throughout the history of humankind in both Western and Eastern traditions. Deconstructed as it must be, romantic/passionate love still compels, and what may yet strain at the soul will be addressed in the next chapter.

For now, we will just touch on a practical question: what criteria should we use to help ourselves or others test what elements of our or their experience of passionate love might be influenced by negative social conditioning of femaleness or maleness. In all unproved theories about gender differences based on sexual difference, one would do well to start with a working hypothesis of an intrinsic equality between the sexes. This hypothesis is predicated on a more general version of equality of persons from which one would also derive an assumption of equality of people of different race. I make no attempt to prove this assumption, and will justify it only by claiming that any other assumption—that one sex or one particular race is intrinsically superior—is almost impossibly problematic. Which sex or what race is entitled to make this evaluation? On what are these values based? Of course, by "equality" I do not imply sameness. I do not have any preconceived notions of *identity*. I intend simply (although not unproblematically) the contextualizing of the issue within the human rights/civil liberties agenda. Additionally, from a psychological point of view, it is also very important to be vigilant that whatever is seen as "feminine" by oneself, the patient, or their particular society or sub-culture is not automatically given a lower psychological value than "masculine". As Hillman demonstrates, the science of the day, including that of our own, is not at all impervious to such unconscious fantasies. From a sociological and political point of view, this relates to the issue of working towards a greater degree of choice for women within the more general constraints of a life lived in society. Importantly, we also need to guard against an over-reaction to the above that would try to devalue what our society currently views as being "masculine". Although this does not happen in the majority of cases, there are certain subcultures where this denigration of the masculine is evident.

In the area of passionate love, in particular, theorists, policy makers, psychotherapists, and others will be empowering women when they further their degree of choice within these limits. Thus, in relationships, some women and men may value passionate love and seek it; others may not do so, and will want to eschew it. In therapy, by exploring what is behind these choices, a person may be helped to develop in the way that best suits them as an individual. In both hetero- and homosexual love relationships, the same primary assumption of equality between the two individual partners should be preserved: relational psychologies, as we have seen, recognize the importance in life of interpersonal relationships and emphasize how mutuality and reciprocity are central ingredients of all healthy pair relationships.

The contribution of the neural sciences discourse

The great advances made in various neuroimaging techniques in particular have led to much recent development in the neurosciences. Some of these bear directly on our theme. As long as we constantly keep in mind that to describe what is going on in the chemistry of the brain is not to have said all that *can* be said on the subject, and do not assume that it is necessarily the most important narrative, we shall not be in danger of a form of materialistic reductionism. In the natural sciences, the discovery that two or more variables occur together does not prove that one is the cause of the other. A clear example of this in affective neuroscience is the contrast between depression following a viral infection and one caused by the loss of a loved one. The symptoms and the specific neurochemistry might be the same in each case (we would expect, for example, reduced serotonin), but in the first, a physical event and the concomitant brain chemistry is clearly causal, and in the second, an emotionally-charged event, the loved one's loss, is clearly causal. To put it succinctly: correlation is not causality!

How the brain is shaped by affection

Gerhardt (2004) explores how conditioning in infancy can actually shape even the "hard-wiring" of a person's brain. She describes how the field of affective neuroscience (those aspects of the scientific study of the nervous system and brain function that include neuro-physiology, biochemistry, psychology, and physics that bear on the phenomenon of feelings/emotions) in particular has made findings that confirm infant studies. In what follows I am drawing on the descriptions Gerhardt provides in her work.

We human beings share with other mammals basic emotional systems corresponding to the primitive brain, that is, the brain stem (subcortex). Fear reactions related to survival, for example, are triggered by the amygdala, which is active at birth. But humans are also a social species, and have the ability to process primitive emotions and to interact in complex ways with others. The orbito-frontal part of the prefrontal cortex (behind the eyes), plus other parts of the prefrontal cortex and anterior cingulate, are responsible for the ability to relate to others. This ability, what we think of as "emotional intelligence", involves the reading of social and emotional cues and empathy (the ability to infer states of mind in others). It is particularly linked to the right side of the brain, the part responsible for seeing the whole pattern, and in visual, spatial, and emotional responses. We could, thus, see this whole associated area of the brain as responsible for making all kinds of *connections*. It is important to note that this part of the brain is not developed at birth, nor does it develop as a matter of course: it is "experience dependent" and *only* develops if there has been intimate social contact between care-giver and baby, such as gentle holding, eye contact, facial expressions, smiles, attuned responses, and so on.

Multiple positive experiences early on in infancy produce brains with more neural connections. We have all our brain cells at birth and do not produce any more, but we need to *connect them up* to make them work for us. Especially between six and twelve months of age, there is a massive burst of synaptic connections in the pre-frontal cortex. These connections provide a dense network of possibilities, the raw material of the mind. Out of this overproduction of connections, patterns start to merge. The most frequent and repetitive experiences start to form well-trodden neural pathways. Once neurons are formed into patterns, they can be used to organize the experience, and make interactions with other human beings more predictable. The baby's brain is categorizing its experiences with other people by noting unconsciously the common features in various events.

Absence of activity causes neurons to atrophy. "Pruning" is when the brain lets go of surplus connections that are not going to be used. One-off experiences leave little trace unless they are emotionally highly-charged. The latter are registered in the amygdala and trigger an automatic response. If there is a chronic lack of positive social interaction with others, the capacity to override these automatic and highly-charged responses may not develop. Postnatally formed links between the prefrontal cortex and the amygdala may be pruned because they are not well established. This means that cognitive processes are then too weak to inhibit flight/fright responses in the infant.

In the baby's second and third years of life, the left brain begins to develop, but this development is based on the earlier development of the right brain. During this time, the processes of paying attention to feelings and expressing them verbally, processing significant memories and putting them into a coherent narrative, and verbal skills are all developed. What is very important for emotional wellbeing is that the left brain's operation should be well connected to the right brain's information.

What this all adds up to is that attachment in the first years of life and beyond actually creates the specifically human brain. In other words, becoming a human being, even at the physical and chemical level, necessitates relationship. In Carroll's words (published on her website):

> The mother's face has particular importance as a "hidden biological regulator" of the infant. The mere perception of emotion on the mother's face creates a resonant emotional state in the baby. Dilation in pupil size, for example, which is associated with interest, engagement and pleasure, makes babies smile more. . . . Studies suggest that expressions can be detected and a positive or negative valence put on them in under a 100 milliseconds (a percept must be held on line for 500 milliseconds to be conscious). The baby is responsive to every dimension of change—in the face, tone, body posture. Intense face to face transactions—traumatic or loving—becoming [become] imprinted in long-term memory and act throughout the lifetime of the individual as an internal regulating object, whether consciously remembered or not. [Carroll, n.d.]

Note how our earlier themes of the importance of maternal mirroring (Winnicott) and of the possibility of early imprinting (Bowlby) are confirmed by these studies. If we review our exploration of the sheer intensity of the feelings surrounding passionate love, this new narrative adds a further dimension of compulsion. If primitive responses such as those triggered by the amygdala are wired to operate well before reason gets a look in, then, when these have been programmed in a pathological way, they will tend automatically to override choices that we might otherwise make.

Of further interest is the fact that changing the neural pathways would seem to require the same degree of emotional intensity (some form of reliving the emotional flavour that was operating at the time the conditioning was laid down) in order to form new (and appropriate) neural pathways. Just as iron must be heated in the first place to shape it, so it must be reheated if the old shape is to be reworked into a new one. It is intensity of feelings that creates the "heat" for such a reworking. This explains why falling in love, whether inside or outside of the consulting room, can be such a catalyst for change.

Having said this, I would like to draw on three of the relatively new hypotheses relating to recent discoveries in neuroscience that, to my mind, shed a lot of light on the phenomenon of passionate love. These are: the idea of "emotional operating systems" within the brain; the specific biochemistry of mate selection; and, finally, what could be termed "the neuroscience of transcendence".

Emotional operating systems

Recent studies in affective neuroscience reveal certain intrinsic, that is, instinctual, emotional action tendencies or "emotional operating systems". These core processes reflect certain evolved emotional action apparatus in the brain that deals with various affective behaviours. Each of these sets of behaviour correlates to certain neurochemical/electrical changes in the brain and can be located around certain clusters of sites in the brain. Watt, in Corrigall and Wilkinson (2003), drawing on the works of Panksepp (1998), and others, outlines the hypothesis that describes a number of these "primary process", "prototypical", or "core" emotional/affective states. These are: seeking and exploratory behaviour; rage ("affective attack"); fear; sexuality; nurturance/maternal care; separation distress/social bonding; and play/joy/social affection. Relevant to our theme are core emotional states of sexuality, separation distress/social bonding, and play/joy/social affection. We can, therefore, begin to focus on the neural mechanisms involved in the selection of a mate and the process of bonding with the mate thus chosen.

Mate selection

Fisher and colleagues, in the field of ethology and anthropology, have researched the neural mechanisms of mate choice (Fisher, Aron, Mashek, Li, & Brown, 2002). Basing her ideas on recent discoveries within the fields of ethology, anthropology, and the relevant neurosciences, Fisher (1998) and (2006) posits the hypothesis that there are three, distinct but overlapping primary emotional systems for mating and reproduction. Each of these is associated with a specific cluster of events in the brain, and each evolved to direct a specific aspect of mammalian reproduction. These are *lust* (or the sex-drive), *attraction*, and *attachment*.

Lust

This emotional system is characterized by the craving for sexual gratification. It is not selective, that is, not specific to a particular individual, but is directed at any member of the same species. It evolved primarily to motivate individuals to seek sexual union with any conspecific and serves the survival of the species as a whole by means of the ensuing reproduction. It is associated primarily with the oestrogens and androgens. In any one instance it is brief, lasting from what might be only a few minutes to a few hours or a few days. Presumably, sexual gratification in any one instance, specifically orgasm, is likely to bring the particular experience of lust to an end.

Attraction

Attraction is the desire for a particular mate. It evolved to facilitate mate selection, furthering the evolution of the species, and enables individuals to focus their mating efforts on preferred conspecifics. It is characterized by increased energy, focused attention on a specific mate, obsessive following, affiliative gestures, possessive mate-guarding, and motivation to win a *preferred* mating partner. It is associated primarily with the catecholamines (dopamine and norepinephrine) and seratonin. It lasts from what might only be days, if the loved one, for example, does not in turn choose the other, to around one or two years, longer if there are obstacles to union. I would speculate that the duration of this system is connected to how long the "courtship" is: if the couple move into close proximity and live together then this system leads more readily into that of attachment (or separation).

Attachment

Attachment, or bonding, known as "companionate love" in humans, serves the evolutionary goal of motivating the pair to form a bond long enough for the time needed for both parents to be together to successfully rear any young produced. It is characterized by behaviours associated with defence of territory, and/or nest building, mutual feeding and grooming, the maintenance of proximity, separation anxiety, shared parental chores, and other affiliative behaviour in mammals, and feelings of calm, security, social comfort, and emotional union in humans. It is associated primarily with the peptides: oxytocin and vasopressin. In humans, Fisher (1998) suggests that this stage often lasts up to around four years, after which any young reared are sufficiently independent for a new mating to occur, but it can, of course, last a lifetime.

It is important to note that attachment is also found in parent–child bonding and friendship bonds, and, hence, is involved in, but not specific to, sexual attraction. It is also important to note that all three systems overlap. Hence, in human beings, sex itself, via orgasm, will release, among other things, more serotonin, which satiates sexual desire at that point but which, in inducing feelings of comfort and wellbeing, can promote attraction and attachment. Again, during sex, oxytocin in released, which in turn can further attachment. Fisher also notes that in humans it is quite possible to experience all three at once: for example, to feel at one and the same time a deep attachment to a long-term partner, a sexual attraction to a specific someone else, and general feelings of lust towards someone entirely unfamiliar but perhaps more generally "sexy". Attraction, of itself, however, is characterized by exclusivity. Fisher suggests that serial monogamy is the general pattern of behaviour in mate selection and breeding for humans.

Fisher and colleagues (2002) cite how, in 1992, anthropologists Jankowiak and Fischer surveyed 166 societies and found evidence of "romantic love" in 147 (i.e., 88.5%) of them. No negative evidence appeared: in the remaining nineteen societies, field scientists "had simply failed to examine this aspect of daily living". They concluded, therefore, that romantic love, which they equate with "passionate love", is a "universal or near-universal human experience . . . a conclusion that suggests that romantic attraction is a distinct emotion-motivation system in the hominid brain" (p. 415). This result confirms the social historians' view, above, which finds evidence against the idea that romantic love or passionate love is merely an invention of Western society. Before we go any further, we would do well to note the distinctions between the meaning of the two terms "passionate" and "romantic". Passionate is a more neutral term, denoting simply that intense feelings connected to sexual attraction are involved. A quick look at a dictionary will reveal that the word "romantic" (from "romance") compounds a whole variety of meanings that include: legendary, chivalric, fictitious or wildly exaggerated, highly imaginative, wondrous or mysterious, and fantastic, including "fantastic" in the sense of truth-distorting. The majority of the definitions that make up the meaning of "romantic" would then seem to denote something considered to be unreal, that is, internal and subjective rather then external and objective. "Romantic love", therefore, would seem to be less of a discernible phenomenon between two people and more an act of imagination expressed especially in human culture and fantasy. We need to keep this distinction clearly in mind and also be very clear which type of phenomenon we are describing. Different connotations will associate consciously or unconsciously to each term.

Having noted the distinction, the study would seem to show that, while models of *marriage* can vary hugely in different societies, with variations which include polygamous, arranged, serial monogamous, and even polyandrous (one wife with more than one husband, as in Tibet), what we are here calling *passionate love* would seem to be present in all societies.

Passionate love and attraction

To return to Fisher's emotional systems for mating and reproduction, passionate love relates most closely to the emotional system of *attraction*. Fisher (2006) writes, "Romantic love begins as an individual comes to regard another as special, even unique". Other typical symptoms include intense focus of attention on the beloved, "aggrandizing the beloved's better traits and overlooking or minimizing his or her flaws" (p. 88). Lovers experience "extreme energy, hyperactivity, sleeplessness, impulsivity, euphoria, and mood-swings. They are goal-oriented and strongly motivated to win the beloved" (*ibid.*). Adversity heightens their passion. Lovers become emotionally dependent on the relationship; they attempt to maintain proximity to their sweetheart and experience separation anxiety when apart; most feel powerful empathy with the beloved and have obsessional thoughts about him or her. Above all is the craving for emotional union with the beloved, which can supersede even their longing for sexual contact. Rejected lovers will go to extraordinary lengths to win back a loved one, and spurned lovers suffer "abandonment rage" and depression which can lead to feelings of hopelessness, lethargy, resignation, and despair. Romantic love is "involuntary, difficult to control, and impermanent" (*ibid.*). Clearly, in the ordinary experience of passionate love, the particularity of the loved one matters a great deal. In practice, there is something both intensely personal and intensely impersonal in the phenomenon, to which we shall return. Last, it is interesting to note that in a survey Fisher (2004) herself conducted of 437 Americans and 402 Japanese, she found that romantic love does not vary significantly with age, gender, sexual orientation, or ethnic group.

We can see from this that there is much about the experience of falling in love that is down to our bodies: our genetic heritage, the hard wiring of our brains, and the biochemistry of mate selection. The fact that these behaviours are rooted in the body's hormonal systems and in the chemistry of the brain, and especially the brain stem, where the more primitive emotions are triggered, gives us an additional explanation for why the experience is so intense and persistent.

The dissolution of the ego

Of great interest is some of the neurological research into the nature of religious and mystical experience. Newberg and colleagues at the University of Pennsylvania used brain imaging techniques on

Tibetan Buddhist monks experienced in meditation (Newberg et al., 2001), and Franciscan nuns experienced in prayer (Newberg, Pourdehnad, Alavi, & d'Aquili, 2003). The conclusions from these studies are described and elaborated upon in Heffern (2001), in Newberg and d'Aquili (2001), and Newberg and Lee (2005). We must note that while results of the experiments followed the empirical approach, the deductions from them are more speculative. To sum up from the different writings: the brain images showed increased activity in the frontal lobes (*the prefrontal cortex*), which the authors call the *attention association area* in the brain. An *association area* is the term for those structures of the brain that gather together neural information from various different parts of the brain. For example, information from a single sense is integrated with that from all the other senses to create rich, multi-dimensional perceptions and tap into memory and emotional centres to allow us to organize and respond to the exterior world in the most complete way possible. The *attention* association area plays a major role in governing complex, integrated bodily movements, and behaviours associated with attaining goals. It is no surprise that the attention association area should be involved in mediation or prayer, since they both involve increased attention, but the experiments also showed decreased activity in the *posterior superior parietal lobe*. This is the area of the brain involved in orientating us in space, "keeping track of which way is up or down, forward or behind, helping us judge distances and angles". A combination of structures in this part of the brain form the *orientation association area*, which "must constantly generate a clear consistent awareness of the physical limits of the self in order for us to function without . . . always stumbling and collapsing" (Heffern, 2001).

The left orientation area is responsible for creating the mental sensation of a limited, physically defined body, while the right orientation area is associated with generating the sense of spatial co-ordinates that provides the matrix in which the body can be orientated (Newberg & d'Aquili, 2001). "In simpler terms, the left OA creates the brain's spatial sense of self, while the right side creates the physical space in which that self can exist" (*ibid.*, p. 28). Scientists know that the orientation association area never rests; so what, the authors ask, would cause the drop in activity in an essential function area of the brain? If the orientation association area is working as hard as ever, but the flow of sensory input is blocked, a neurological phenomenon known as *deafferentation*, then possibly the brain would not be able to make the distinction between self and everything that is not the self. The two scientists posited that deafferentation is responsible for the experience of a unitary state.

The "aesthetic–religious" continuum

d'Aquili and Newberg (2000) describe how they defined nine different *primary epistemic* (or "knowing") *states*. These are nine primary ways of sensing reality. The scientists divided the nine epistemic states into two categories: six fall into the first category, which groups together those states involving the perception of *discrete entities* (such as various objects, space and time, self and not self) and regular relationships between elements of that reality (such as cause and effect.) The other three fall into the second category, which groups together rare states that relate to what they term "Absolute Unitary Being", which is a state, "usually arising out of profound meditation, characterized by absolute unity", in which there is no perception of space or time and in which "even the self–other dichotomy is obliterated" (*ibid.*, p. 43). Of the first six states, three are inherently stable (the other three are inherently unstable, e.g., drug or psychosis or dementia induced). The former stable primary epistemic states are categorized by the feeling quality pertaining to each state: first, neutral affect: *baseline reality*—the ordinary waking state; second, positive affect, with a "Cosmic" type of consciousness, and third, negative affect.

Thus, the second of the three stable knowing states

> involves the same discrete entities and regularities as the ordinary baseline state, but it also involves an elated sense of well-being and joy, in which the universe is perceived to be fundamentally good and all its parts are sensed to be related in a unified whole. In this state one usually has a sense of purposefulness to the universe and to one's place in the universe. [*ibid.*, p. 42]

These nine primary epistemic states would seem to make up a spectrum, or continuum, of unitary states with diversity at one end of the spectrum and unity at the other. As one moves across this continuum away from baseline reality, the sense of unity increasingly transcends the sense of diversity. Near, but not at, the "diverse" end of the spectrum, close to baseline reality, is the experience of positive aesthetics, where positive affect suffuses one's sense of reality. The sense of wholeness, here, is greater than the diversity of the parts. This would be the case in the appreciation of a beautiful sunset, a work of art, or a piece of music. As one moves along the spectrum, towards the sense of greater unity, one moves out of the realm of aesthetics and into a realm that is aptly described as religious experience.

Of relevance to our theme is d'Aquili's and Newberg's suggestion that romantic love might be a transitional phase leading from aesthetic experiences into experiences, towards the other (unitary) end of the spectrum, of numinosity, or religious awe. As one continues along this spectrum beyond cosmic consciousness, one moves into various "trance" states in which there is a progressive blurring of the boundaries between entities until one finally moves into what they term "Absolute Unitary Being". In absolute unitary being, one is in another primary epistemic state since absolute unitary being is characterized by absolute unity. There are no longer any discrete entities that relate to each other. The boundaries of entities within the world disappear, and even the self–other dichotomy is totally obliterated. In absolute unitary being there is no extension of space or duration of time. If it is suffused with positive affect, it is interpreted as an experience of God or the mystical union; if with neutral affect, as the void or Nirvana. d'Aquili and Newberg postulated that moving up this continuum is at least partially due to progressive deafferentation; total deafferentation resulting in the total and absolute unitary experience of absolute unitary being. SPECT images confirmed this.

I would like to single out an important statement made in the above paper: "The whole point of most spiritual–mystical experiences is for the self to have a sense of being fundamentally and essentially related to some aspect of whatever ultimate reality might be" (ibid., p. 47).

And in an interview (Heffern, 2001), Newberg stated, "We believe the neurological machinery of transcendence may have arisen from the neural circuitry that evolved for mating and sexual experience". This process, by which various human brain functions evolved from the brain functions of more "primitive" animals, has been termed "encaphalization". Heffern, referring to Newberg and d'Aquili's writings, suggests, "Mystics use terms like *bliss, rapture, ecstasy, exaltation.* It's no accident that this is also the language of sexual arousal". Although sex and prayer are clearly different experiences, they would seem to *use similar neural pathways.* The wiring in the human brain that evolved for the functions related both to mystical experiences or unitary states of being and to the human experience of falling in love would, thus, seem to be complex and highly sophisticated modifications of primitive mating operating systems. The same note is sounded, but at a higher octave.

Another important thing to note is that functions of the attention area and the orientation association area appear very similar to the various functions of the ego as described by Jung (1959b, pars 1–12). For Jung, the ego is not a thing in itself, but is a function which is associated with our bodily sense of self, with both internal and external physical perceptions, memories, thoughts, feelings, and ideas, the experience of choice, volition, and so on. The ego, of course, functions as a centre of consciousness. Yet, this sense of "I-ness" is not only the condition for consciousness, but also must, of course, be itself a content of consciousness. In this sense, we could say that the ego complex is a kind of illusion: an illusion of a fragmented self (the conscious self) separated out from the totality which is the Self.

To return to the phenomenon of deafferentation, it would seem to be the case that falling in love, positioned as it is midway along the aesthetic–religious continuum, is a state of awareness at a midpoint between the ordinary losing of a sense of separate ego in a beautiful sunset or piece of music and the beginnings of states of awareness of unitary being, which have the potential to lead to those described as absolute unitary being. Perhaps, as we shall see later, falling in love could provide a means of initiation into such a state. Losing one's sense of a separate self is not the same as losing one's ego altogether, and there is a danger in confusing the positive loss of a sense of a separate, alienated self in falling in love with loss of the *ego* as such: the bliss or surrender of the dissolution of ego boundaries in an experience of unitary being could very easily be mistakenly identified as surrender to the loved one. A subtle but crucially important distinction must be made between the two. I shall explore this distinction in Chapter Six.

Bliss

We can now return to our theme of bliss with this scientific point of view in mind, but it must be noted that my thinking here, elaborated from scientific research, is highly speculative in nature.

A fruitful field is the neuroscience of addiction. Research has been done (Shaffer, 2008) on "process or activity addictions" (as opposed to psychoactive substance-using addictions), such as pathological gambling and "excessive sexual behaviours". In process or activity addictions, repetitive and excessive patterns of emotionally stirring experiences would seem to be a more important factor than the object of these acts. In addictions to psychoactive substances, the substance itself is the most important factor. Despite this difference, it was shown that in the case of process additions, the same areas of the brain are involved as those that respond to drugs such as cocaine. A "love addict" may be hooked to a "high" based on a cocktail of adrenaline and dopamine (which is involved in cocaine addiction) and seek this again and again in much the same way as the other addictions. The notion of "love addiction" may be of great help in understanding the more pathological traits of behaviour in love relationships, such as Don Juanism in men or women. The same chemistry may also help us to understand the degree of compulsivity involved in the normal spectrum of falling in love. See, for example, Fisher (1992, 1994) on the possible role of naturally occurring neurochemicals such as PEA.

I was fascinated to learn of the discovery of an altogether different neurochemical (Senese, 1998). Scientists researching the positive effects of marijuana had been looking for an explanation as to why the brain was receptive to the drug. Senese explains that, as we know, communication between the various nerve cells in the brain occurs when various "key" molecules in nerve cells are released and intercepted by specific receptors in the surface of other nerve cells downstream. The active ingredient of marijuana—THC (tetrahydrocannibol)—does not occur naturally in the body: it must, therefore, mimic a natural messenger molecule. This messenger molecule turned out to be arachidonyl ethanolamide, later called "anandamide" from the Sanskrit word for bliss. Anandamide elicits virtually all of the known effects of cannabis. Much more research needs to be done, but, should the bliss of falling in love be partly explained at the neurological level by the natural release of such key molecules, then we could learn much about the biochemical underpinnings of such states. Anandamide, for example, not only dilates blood vessels and bronchial tubes in the lungs, thereby decreasing blood pressure and pulse rate and having an important calming effect, it also has anticancer properties and possibly mitigates pain. It affects appetite and, what is also extremely interesting, some evidence suggests that it might play a role in the memory: it is possibly a forgetting chemical. Some have suggested that its presence in the brain is increased by the practice of meditation.

There are clear parallels here with the "highs" of falling in love: the experience of bliss, the state of being more inured to pain, even perhaps the forgetfulness of a person in love. Strangest of all is the role anandamide plays outside of the brain, where it acts as a chemical messenger between the embryo and the uterus during implantation of the embryo in the uterine wall. "As such, it is one of the first communications that occurs between mother and child" (Senese, 1998). Research in neuroscience might confirm what psychoanalysis hit upon phenomenologically: the first intoxicating love affair would then indeed be that between mother and child! The states of "oceanic bliss" experienced in the womb may well be duplicated (although more toxically) in recreational drugs, in falling in love, and in meditation.

In conclusion, the natural sciences, ethology, biology, and the neurosciences, give us a language to explore passionate love from the point of view of our physical and biological nature with a brain chemistry wired towards our survival both as individuals and as a species. Because it serves survival, that "hard-wiring" cannot, nor should, be readily overridden. The strength of the various emotional operating systems will function in great measure as unalterable determinates of our behaviour in relation to attraction to others. We are embodied beings and, as such, live with certain givens that we share with other mammals. The particular way we have of being human, therefore, operates as a refined variation on a basic theme.

The limitations of the scientific discourse

The sciences, both the natural and the social sciences, show us the value for the fully functioning adult of those instincts and social structures relating to the survival of the human race, to mate-choice, and the intimate sharing of life with a companion. Yet, when all is said and done, we still seem not to have said enough. If passionate love has been crucially formed by early childhood influences and is highly influenced by biological, neural, and social mechanisms, is that then all there is to it? Poetry, for one, would seem to suggest that more must be involved; that there seems to be in the soul of the human being a longing for something that is not altogether fully explained by psychological conditioning and pure survival instincts. In the next chapter, we shall explore what this is.

PART I

(C) What we may be: individuation

CHAPTER FOUR

The teleological discourse

We have not yet addressed questions as to why falling in love seems to transport us into another dimension. Why can it evoke what seem to be our deepest or most spiritual longings? There exist other psychological narratives that do not define what we are only in terms of what has conditioned us, nor simply in terms of our social and genetic aims as adults, but which look to, or also look to, what we might become. Jung's writings constitute some of the foremost contributions in this field, and his ideas are relevant to our theme. However, they also need to be recontextualized. Most valuable in this context is Jung's description of a process that he termed "individuation". Falling in love may be a means of individuating. By individuation, Jung did not mean the process of becoming an ego, as in Mahler and colleagues' definition (Mahler, Pine, & Bergman, 1975) and I will begin with his definition.

Individuation

Individuation is the term used "to denote the process by which a person becomes a psychological 'individual', that is, a separate, indivisible unity or 'whole'" (Jung, 1959a, par. 490). It is that process within the human being that causes them to become what they uniquely have the potential to be. Individuation is not individualism: the latter is reactive, asserting one's differences *against* that of the community; the former is driven by inner forces: the call to become who one is, which can have the consequence of taking one away from the herd, the merely collective existence. However, presumably precisely because it is indeed an instinct, Jung asserts that individuation does not take us away from the experience of being a human being among other human beings: ultimately, it leads a person to become more of a human being, a full member of the human race. Individuation, thus, always has two main aspects: "in the first place it is an internal and subjective process of integration, and in the second it is an equally indispensible process of objective relationship" (1954b, par. 448). Jung relates this second aspect to the "kinship libido" which is connected to an "endogamous instinct". The term "endogamy", in anthropology, means marrying within (the consanguineous marriage), and, thus, denotes the tendency to relate to kindred spirits. Psychologically speaking, endogamy is the union of divided components of the personality; in other words, the cohering of a fragmented self into the one self. Its opposite is "exogamy", meaning marrying outside (non-consanguineous marriage), which Jung uses to denote the tendency to relate to strangers. Psychologically speaking, it is the tendency to fragment the self. Both in society and within the psyche, endogamy and exogamy are two opposing tendencies each indispensable and each needing to be in tension with the other in order to limit the each one's extent. This is the tension between a tendency to come together and to fly apart. An analogy in physics is with centripetal and centrifugal forces. In his book, *The Psychology of the Transference* (1954b, par. 445) Jung writes,

> To the extent that the transference is projection and nothing more, it divides quite as much as it connects. But experience teaches that there is one connection in the transference which does not break off with the severance of projection. That is because there is an extremely important instinctive factor behind it: the kinship libido. This has been pushed so far into the background by the unlimited expansion of the exogamous tendency that it can find an outlet, and a modest one at that, only within the immediate family circle, and

sometimes not even there, because of the quite justifiable resistance to incest. While exogamy was limited by endogamy, it resulted in a natural organization of society which has entirely disappeared today. Everyone is now a stranger among strangers. Kinship libido—which could still engender a satisfying feeling of belonging together . . . has long been deprived of its object. But, being an instinct, it is not to be satisfied by any mere substitute such as a creed, party, nation, or state. It wants the *human* connection. That is the core of the whole transference phenomenon, and it is impossible to argue it away, *because relationship to the self is at once relationship to our fellow man, and no one can be related to the latter until he is related to himself.* [my italics]

Not only is there no "either/or" for Jung, but relationship to self is, at one and the same time, relationship to our fellow human beings and vice versa.

We long, rightly, for the human connection; we long for it with our fellow human beings and we long for it within. I do not think it is stating too much to maintain that deep within every person is a kind of homesickness, a yearning to belong. This is, at one and the same time, a longing to be a part of the universe and to be whole in oneself. The opposite is alienation, when one neither belongs to the universe nor is at home within oneself. I would suggest that falling in love can be an expression of that longing: that through relationship I might find that I belong in the world, and I might also come home to myself. This deeply longed-for goal—that of relationship to others and to oneself, at one and the same time macrocosmic and microcosmic wholeness—has been symbolized throughout the ages by the object which is prized beyond all others: the Water of Eternal Life, the Holy Grail, the Golden Apples of the Sun, and the Philosopher's Stone. It is no accident that the fairy tales that describe the quest for such an object end not only with the hero or heroine finding and bringing back the object, but also with a marriage. The human connection is both the means and the end.

Each person's path of individuation, of becoming whole, is unique to them, but each person's path also has elements in common with everyone else. Certain key elements within the psyche need to be integrated over a person's lifetime, and these are: the repudiated part of the self, the *Shadow*; the contrasexual aspect of the self, the *Animus* or *Anima*, which I have termed simply the

Inner Partner; and the total personality, *the Self*. But the order is fluid, and in falling in love, for example, the Shadow might be the last of the psychic contents to be constellated. All three elements have both a personal and a non-personal aspect to them: they comprise a complex formed around an archetypal core. Hence, I shall first give an outline of what Jung means by an *archetype*.

Archetypes

One of the ideas in depth psychology that is unique to Jung, and can help us greatly with our understanding of passionate love, is the notion of a collective area of the psyche: that is, what we share with others by virtue of our membership of the human race. Jung observed that in the myths, folk tales, religious rites, and initiations from all over the world, definite motifs recur. The same motifs are to be found in the fantasies, dreams, and psychotic delusions of contemporary people. These motifs he termed archetypal ideas. He posited that they derived from archetypes that would seem to be inherited. They are connected to certain life experiences that all human beings have in common. Each one of us is conceived by a mother and begotten by a father, and gestates in the womb, even if we are not brought up by either parent. We are born, we reach puberty, experience sexual attraction, have the capacity to conceive or beget children of our own, whether or not we do so, and, over time, have to confront suffering, ageing, and, eventually, death. These life experiences, for which we are equipped via our instincts, and which are encountered and acted out by human beings time and time again over millennia, both derive from, and in turn shape, the archetypes. An archetype itself has no form, but is a *tendency* to form certain ideas or mental representations. Jung gives as an analogy the innate structure of the different salts, which always gives rise to a specific form of crystal, for example, the rhomboid copper sulphate crystal. This is always so, even if any one crystal is not perfectly rhomboid. An even better example might be the ubiquitous hexagonal pattern of the snowflake, which, through each individual flake, can reveal untold variations on this single pattern.

Let us compare this idea with what we have seen already with respect to behavioural patterns. As Bowlby (1969) notes,

> Instinctive behaviour is not inherited: what is inherited is a poten-
> tial to develop certain sorts of system, termed here behavioural
> systems, both the nature and the forms of which differ in some
> measure according to the particular environment in which develop-
> ment takes place. [pp. 70–71]

> For example, a bird of a species that habitually nests in trees may
> nest on cliffs when no trees offer: buzzards in Norway are an exam-
> ple. [p. 70]

It is thus not the content of "tree" itself which is part of the nesting instinct for this species of bird, but something more like the "tendency to attain a safe height". In other words, it is the *general pattern*, not the *detail of content*, that is predetermined.

Bowlby restricts himself to describing certain types of instinc-tive *behaviour*; Jung sees a correlation between these behavioural patterns and the instincts, ideation, and imagery. The unconscious seems to be structured in such a way as to produce certain key clus-ters of images and ways of thinking in the human species. Affective neuroscience, with its notion of emotional operating systems, as we have seen, may well indicate the validity of this hypothesis. Exam-ples of archetypes are the Wise Old Man or Woman, the Mother, the Father, the Child, the archetype of Rebirth, etc. It is not hard to see how all of these examples might derive from the basic human expe-riences of old age, parenting and being parented, and the birth and death cycle of life.

We do not "have" an archetype; since an archetype is always supraordinate to the ego it is more true to say that the archetype "has us". In the myths of classical Greece, they are the mighty gods who play with human destinies, to whom the puny human being (the ego) must pay due tribute. This is why we do not walk into with grace, or even "rush in" like fools, but "fall in" love. Since the archetype of the Inner Beloved, or the Inner Partner, is often the first to be constellated in passionate love, we can look at this first.

The Inner Partner

Traditionally, the internal figure of the Lover, which is projected on to a person's outer lovers, has been taken to be of the opposite gender to them. Jung calls these inner figures the Animus, or the Anima. Growing up as a person of either male or female sex, and within the definitions of gender that our society allows to each of us, has the effect that qualities seen as belonging to the opposite sex are likely to be pushed into the unconscious where they reside until attraction to the opposite sex can awake at least something of what is repressed. Both nature and nurture will determine what qualities are disavowed in this way. The contrasexual inner figure will be based on the interface between an individual's conditioning and what feels naturally alien to them as a gendered self. This figure, then, is in part an amalgam of all those qualities that have been disavowed and are seen only as belonging to the opposite sex. Jung called all those the aspects of the man that he is not allowed to live out, or does not allow himself to live out by virtue of being a man, the "Anima" and all those aspects of the woman that she is not allowed to live out, or does not allow herself to live out by virtue of being a woman, the "Animus". Psychological wholeness is based on an integration of both these aspects: symbolically, a "marriage" of the "masculine" and "feminine".

But feminist thinking has posed the question: what *is* innate femininity and what is innate masculinity? What are simply stereotypes and fantasies about the different sexes and what are truly universal tendencies in men and women? Using postmodern and feminist approaches, Young-Eisendrath (1997) has written extremely helpfully on this theme, and has taken up the idea of there being a distinction between sex, as a biological given, and gender as a social and cultural construct. I recommend her work (see also Young-Eisendrath [1999]). We can examine this briefly here, but there is not the space to take this up in detail. I will write more of this elsewhere.

Young-Eisendrath makes good use of Jung's notion of a "complex", a whole conglomeration of feeling-toned ideas clustered around an archetype. She distinguishes the contrasexual complex, in which the "Gendered Other" will carry all the fantasies and projections a person will put on to a member of the opposite sex, and the contrasexual archetype. Although Jung referred to *archetypes* of the masculine and feminine, he made the mistake of going on to describe the Anima archetype, in particular, in terms of its content, and so was really describing a man's (and his own) Anima complex. Young-Eisendrath shows that what is of real value in Jung's concept of Animus and Anima as archetypes is the idea that each is responsible for very *tendency itself to polarize*. From Jung's theory of archetypes, we can see that the extent to which Animus–Anima are personal is the extent to which they will be highly culturally conditioned. The Animus or Anima in the psyche is conditioned by the individual's own personal history, which, in turn, is shaped by time and place. Conversely, to the extent to which these figures are archetypal (that is, universal), they must, by definition, hold *in all places and at all times*. If we explore the Animus and Anima as archetypes, and, hence, as related to the instincts rather than to conditioned stereotypes, and, furthermore, see them as not pertaining to individual men and women, then, from a psychological point of view as distinct from the physical one, we not only may, but ultimately *must*, help ourselves to whatever characteristics or qualities are of value rather than limiting ourselves only to those which fit the gender stereotypes. Greater (inner) choice (i.e., flexibility) arises in a situation in which one is not prevented by conditioning from availing oneself of, and developing, those qualities that are seen as only properly belonging to the opposite sex. The more integrated a person in that respect, the more he or she will manifest a quality of versatility in relation to gender stereotypes.

However, psychological narratives have tended to pathologize those instances where the Inner Lover figure is not of the opposite gender, as in homosexual love. In order to do proper justice to homosexual love relationships, we need to separate out two aspects of the Inner Lover archetype, that of the *Kindred Spirit* and that of the *Stranger*. In heterosexual love, the strangeness of the beloved is mostly carried by the otherness of the beloved's opposing sex, which can carry all the lover's projections to do with opposite gender. Kinship will be experienced in seeing similar qualities outside of contrasexual projections. In homosexual love, the strangeness of the beloved will be carried by qualities other than sex, and any gender-type roles may or may not be fixed, while the sense of kinship is carried by the sameness of the other's gender. Hence, if we try to put the issue of falling in love in a general way, we could say that the attraction to the other exhibited in falling in love is experienced as an attraction *both* towards that in the other which is *similar* to oneself *and* to that which is *different*. Many writers, such as Pickering (2008), emphasize only the value of exogamous attraction, that is, of unlike to unlike: an attraction to what is "Other". Yet, as Jung emphasized, exogamy must be limited by endogamy, that is, an attraction of like to like, to a beloved who is similar to us. Those elements which we see in the beloved and experience as being *unlike* ourselves provoke a sense of mystery and complementarity , and those elements which we see in them and experience as being *like* ourselves provoke empathy and identification. When there is a genuine *affinity* with a loved one, I see what is similar to me in the other. If I am to see accurately, I need to take back projections of *complementarity*, that is, of otherness (alterity), which do not belong to the other. In doing this, I free the other from having to possess those qualities that are experienced as missing (not conscious or not-yet-developed) in me. When there is a genuine experience of *alterity* with a loved one, I see what is different from me in the other. To see accurately, I need to take back my projections of *identity*, that is, of sameness (similarity), which do not belong to the other, and free them from having to possess the same qualities as me. I would maintain that elements of both similarity and alterity must be present, and present in the "right" balance, that is, right for the individual, in order for them to experience attraction. It might even be that the balance shifts over a person's development: I think in adolescence, in general, *differences* are experienced as more desirable, whereas in maturity, the quality of the "soul-mate", a sense of *likeness*, is experienced as more desirable. Compensation must also be accounted for. A person who has married someone obviously like themselves might, in a second marriage, be more drawn to someone less like themselves or vice versa.

It is the discovery of real likeness and real unlikeness that gives such value to both inner and outer relationships, and it is similarly the illusion of similarity and the illusion of alterity that can be so destructive of good inner and outer relationships. But it is important to note that it is not the projection itself that is destructive (projections can serve realization); it is the maintaining of a projection past the point at which we need to take it back that is destructive. At first, projections serve development, and only after a certain point do they become defensive.

So let us, for our purposes in exploring the phenomenon of falling in love, simply take the radical but hugely important step of removing the descriptions that involve a specifically gendered nature to the archetypes of Animus/Anima. This leaves us with the universal figure of the Inner Partner, the Beloved, the significant other, who is one's soul mate, one's "other half". This will, as a simple matter of empirical fact, be a figure of the opposite sex for heterosexuals and of the same sex for homosexuals. In each case, and for both men and women, I suggest, this figure will be a bridge to their own unconscious and, as we have seen, will tend to polarize around sameness and difference, self and other. If the archetype of the Inner Partner is constellated by an attraction to an outer beloved, then falling in love with a real man or woman can also be a gateway to the lover's unconscious. If the experience of falling in love is constellated by an attraction to the Inner Partner, then this inner attraction can also be a gateway to human passionate love. We can see from this how erotic love can be a critical means towards becoming whole.

The Inner Lover as bridge to the unconscious

In a great variety of myths, fairy-tales, and legends, the coming together of two lovers involves a crossing of the boundary between of two distinct worlds. The Greek myths contain very many stories of a god mating with a human woman or a goddess mating with a human male. Many legends have the theme of the pairing of a human with some fairy-like figure from the animal world. In the Celtic stories about the silkie, the fairy lover is a seal by day and a man or woman only by night; the fairy-tale behind the ballet *Swan Lake* has the love between a mortal man and a Swan maiden as its theme; the story of Undine has the pairing of man and water sprite; there is the pairing of a faery woman and a human man in very many other Celtic legends, and in the story of *Beauty and the Beast*, it is of a human woman and a beast figure.

It is also interesting to note how many fantasy novels or films of that genre continue this theme: in Tolkein's *The Lord of the Rings* (1968) trilogy there is the love affair between the man, the hero Aragorn, and the elfin lady Arwen. Neither can live in the other's world without a sacrifice. The film *Ladyhawke* tells a story by

Khmara (1985) of a love between a knight, Captain Etienne Navarre, and the lady Isabeau d'Anjou. They have been cursed by an evil bishop, so that Navarre is human by day, but takes the form of a wolf by night, while Isabeau is a hawk by day and a lady only by night. The two would, thus, seem doomed never to meet. In Philip Pullman's trilogy *His Dark Materials* (1995), his heroine, Lyra, and hero, Will, come, quite literally, from two different worlds, Will from our world and Lyra from a parallel world. Each can only meet by the creation of an unnatural rift between the two worlds. I will take up this story in more detail later in this chapter. There are countless other examples of love stories where the lovers come from two different realms and where this creates insuperable, or nearly insuperable, obstacles to their love. In these myths, it would seem that the beloved is attractive to the lover precisely because of the difference between their worlds, and yet, the more different their worlds are, the more each has to adapt to, or to some extent assimilate, the other's world in order to be able to have a future life together.

So what is the meaning behind this theme, which repeats itself time and again in such stories? It is a question that Jung (1954a, 1956a, 1959) and other writers after him (see, for example, Jung, E., 1955; von Franz, 1970, 1974, 1977, 1997, 2002; Johnson, 1983) have addressed. That the lovers are animals, or elemental or fairy beings from a non-human world, symbolizes that these are figures from the unconscious.

The fairy story "Day Boy and Night Girl", by MacDonald (1961), tells of the love between a boy who has been brought up to see only daylight and a girl who has been brought up to see only the night. Psychologically speaking, day represents the world of the conscious (the tale is told from the man's perspective) and night the world of the unconscious. Since the girl, the boy's anima figure, is awake only at night and he only by day, the two can never meet. Twilight represents a transitional space, the boundaries between the world of the unconscious and that of the conscious. It is only here, in this liminal space at the threshold between the two worlds, that the two lovers can meet. In other tales, that liminal space might be the sea-shore, the boundary between land and sea, the dark wood or forest, and so on. In *Ladyhawke*, this threshold place is at the time of an eclipse of the sun by the moon, when neither day nor night predominates. In Pullman's tale, the point of intersection is represented by a rent in the barrier between the two worlds.

Crossing the boundary between the two worlds is always a perilous feat: the human male, for example, could be, and in some stories is, trapped forever in the faery world. In Pullman's tale, for the two lovers to be able to remain together either the rent between the Will's and Lyra's worlds must be kept open, which would allow the life energy of all the worlds to leak out, or one of them must live in the other's world. Lyra is prepared to make that sacrifice, but Will cannot let her, as she would simply fade away, and it is his very love for her that could not allow that to happen. Conversely, the mortal man who loves the water sprite or fairy risks the danger of drowning in her element, or losing his youth while dwelling in her world.

In the tragic tales, accommodation to, or reconciliation with, the alien world is not possible, and it is the very difference between these two worlds that forms the insurmountable obstacle to the final consummation of love. This means that the two lovers are unable to accommodate their antithetical natures and, if we read the tale as symbolic of the psychological state of an individual, that conscious and unconscious are too disparate. This is the case in the Pullman tale, in Hans Andersen's *The Little Mermaid* (1836), and so on. In happier tales, such as *Beauty and the Beast*, *Amor and Psyche*, and *Ladyhawke*, for example, the lovers find a way of being able to live together. But, even in these happy tales, great trials and suffering are required before either hero or heroine or both achieve the task.

Perhaps most interesting of all is a particular variation on this theme in two different, but related, fairy stories. In these, we are given alternative endings: one tragic, one happy. We are familiar with the tragic ending of the tale on which *Swan Lake* is based. The central theme is to be found in a Swedish tale, "The Swan Maiden" (Hofberg, 1890). In this story, a young man hunting catches sight of three swans, who set aside their feathers to become three maidens who bathe and play in the water and then fly away. He falls in love with the youngest, and manages to capture her by stealing her feathered robes. He refuses to return them, and the two become man and wife. They live happily together until one day he shows her the swan feathers, whereupon she puts them on and flies away for ever.

However, a lesser known tale, also called "The Swan Maiden" (Jacobs, 1916), has an almost identical central theme. In this tale, there are seven swan maidens. Again, the hunter wins the youngest for himself by taking her feathered clothes away from her when she bathes. They marry and have two children, a boy and a girl. One day, the little girl is playing hide and seek and comes across her mother's swan feathers. The swan maiden recovers them and immediately departs. In this tale, however, the young man does not rest content with her loss, but travels far and wide to find the land "East of the Sun and West of the Moon", where she lives with her father. After many adventures, he finds the place and boldly asks her father if he may leave with his bride. He is shown seven identical maidens all "dressed in their robes of feathers and looking each like all the rest". The young man takes each maiden in turn by the right hand, and from the hand alone is able to recognize his wife. The father thereupon loads them with gifts and the two depart to live happily ever after.

In the story, a charming detail is afforded us: the young man wins his bride again because he is able to recognize the forefinger of her right hand by the needle marks from sewing their children's clothes. In other words, he may win her back because the archetype has been humanized or incarnated. The young man truly deserves her now, because he knows her so well and in such detail. Whereas before he had simply stolen her from her world, now he has properly won her. If we strip the tale of its gender stereotyping, the marks, whether in a female or male Inner Partner, represent the everyday, mundane acts of love that come from the care of the children that they have together. A contemporary take on these tasks might be cooking the supper, putting out the rubbish, going out to work to provide for the family, taking the children to school, any of which might be shared. In our inner relationship, just as in an outer one, the glories of falling in love must be transmuted into everyday commitment. The swan-maid's father (a regressive element in the psyche) is now compelled to let her go, and the two lovers are allowed to bridge the difference between the two worlds and live as husband and wife.

Thus, perhaps, we may even infer that the tragic tales remain tragic *because they are stories of incomplete individuation*. In workshops, using active imagination or dream figures, I have worked with participants to (re)encounter this inner figure and see what the nature of their relationship with them is like. It can be valuable for each to explore through imagination what is the *smallest* first step they might take towards removing the obstacles between them and their inner beloved. For one man, it was a gesture as tiny and yet as tender as removing a strand of hair from her eyes.

The Shadow

The feeling of *sexual attraction* to what is an unknown aspect of myself and, therefore, experienced as not-self, is not (initially) fused with the feeling quality of *aversion*. The archetype of the Inner Lover may overlap with, but is distinct from, the archetype of the adversary, the enemy or love rival. When we fall in love, it is our rival in love, the "other woman", or "other man" who often carries that Shadow archetype for us.

The shadow, briefly, is Jung's term for that part of our personality that lies beyond our conscious awareness. By definition, it forms a part of the unconscious. This means that *we will not and cannot be aware of it at any one time.* What constitute the shadow are those parts of the personality that do not fit in with our idea of ourselves, with how we would like to see ourselves. This may be because we do not accept such traits, due to our own character and preferences. It can also be due to environmental influences, especially early conditioning: what was not acceptable to parents, our peers, school teachers, society, even a whole nation. For example, the British "stiff upper lip", perhaps now less prevalent than formerly, arose from the literal stiffening of the mouth in response to repeated, mostly unconscious attempts to subdue tears. Tears, especially in men, had formed part of the shadow because these did not fit in the ideas of male "toughness".

By working on ourselves, we can become aware of aspects of our shadow and, thus, more aware of those occasions when the shadow has taken over. These aspects may be acknowledged, accepted, and taken on board, and, thus, become part of the conscious personality. However, Jung stresses that we can never exhaust the unconscious: there is always more that can be integrated. At any one point, no matter how much work we may have done on ourselves, there is always a shadow, that is, always some aspect of ourselves that we may be keeping at bay. What can be changed is our attitude, our readiness to acknowledge and integrate the shadow, and, hence, we can become better at recognizing those little clues that indicate the presence of shadow material. Then what was previously an obstacle within the psyche can become a resource. Buried with this shadow are also much of the vitality, spontaneity, and resourcefulness of the psyche.

So, is there a particular relationship between the process of integrating the shadow and the experience of falling in love? In the first flush of love, when a positive, complementary aspect of self is being projected, there often appears to be some major aspect of difference that is a fundamental part of the attraction. Later, as the relationship develops, and particularly if it develops to the point of sharing life together, what I think of as the "over the toast and marmalade" point, then the negative elements of what one accurately sees in the other, or of what one might be projecting on to them, come into play. It has often been noted that the very aspect of the other that was first found to be most attractive—often those aspects seen as the complementary to one's own nature (as consciously perceived)—can, over time, be the very aspect that most palls. The strong decisive lover may, with familiarity, begin to seem a bully, the sweetly obliging wife a doormat, and so on. When we fall in love, we are in love with the "otherness" of the other; when we continue to love we can be most irritated by that very otherness of the other. These facts relate to the stages that, strictly speaking, come after that of passionate love and are very well explored in detail in Pickering (2008). In the passionate stage of love, the shadow is evoked most of all by virtue of the sheer intensity of the experience. The primitive child-related aspects of the self that we explored in the first two chapters, the rage, jealousy, hatred, possessiveness, envy, sado-masochism, and so on, are very much the sort of feelings that will be the contents of the personal shadow.

One mature woman, Eileen, at the beginning of a new relationship discovered a depth of love that she had not thought possible. The experience also opened her up to a degree of need of which she had previously been unaware. The overwhelming nature of those needs brought out an aspect of her unconscious that she likened to Mrs Rochester, the madwoman in the attic, unkempt, uncared for, ready to wreak her revenge on Jane Eyre, her constrained self (see Brontë, 1847). This "crazy" self was an aspect of herself she did not want to own. After much work with this figure, Eileen was eventually able, in active imagination, to invite the madwoman down from the attic and into her living room. In doing so, she noticed a particular and striking detail: the madwoman's hair was unkempt. From this tiny clue Eileen recognized a connection between this figure and herself as a child. Experiences of early neglect had been internalized in the form of an inner child figure that she was now herself inadvertently abandoning. Eileen found herself filled with a new tenderness and pity for the madwoman/child figure and, in the imagined scenario, wanted to let her live freely and not shut away as if an animal. Charlotte Brontë's novel *Jane Eyre* can be read as a very accurate description of the workings of the shadow in a woman in love. For an illuminating literary analysis of Bertha Rochester as Jane Eyre's "dark double", see Gilbert and Gubar (1979.)

If the relationship is allowed to develop, then it is more likely that it is the beloved themselves, rather than a real or imagined rival, who begins to carry the shadow for the lover. We have seen above that the very thing that can attract a person to another, in the first instance, can be the very thing that later gets on that person's nerves. When this is happening, we have the phenomenon of "falling out of love". Of course, falling out of love is different from continuing to love a person but ceasing to be "in love" with them. This last may allow for a more realistic image of the person, without the idealizing projections, and which may, therefore, leave companionate love intact. It is, further, not the same as growing out of a relationship over time, which may or may not arise from seeing the other more realistically. In "falling out of love" the beloved's shadow (and, therefore, the lover's own shadow in its projected form) is repudiated, either one or both partners being unable to come to terms with it. For an excellent account of how a long-term commitment to relationship can be a means of individuation through the integration of shadow material, see *Marriage Dead or Alive* (Guggenbühl-Craig, 1977).

The Self

The drive to individuation manifests in a person as a drive to wholeness operating from within the unconscious. Jung (1959a) uses the term "Self" to indicate the sum total of psychic phenomena, conscious and unconscious. Because it includes an unknown factor (what is in the unconscious), the self must elude definition, but it functions also as an ordering centre within the psyche. This self-regulating function parallels the body's own drive to health and balance. Figuratively, therefore, Jung describes the Self as being like both the area of a circle and its centre. I will use the term "Self archetype" to connote that aspect of the Self which is a fluid, non-fixed attempt at coherence and integrity based on the Self as function (see Young-Eisendrath & Hall [1991]), and coin the term "Self figure" for when the aspect of Self as "numinous Other" is to the fore. However, for an excellent defence of diversity and a contemporary description of the psyche as also plural, see Samuels (1989).

In clinical practice, this drive of the psyche to wholeness—or, given the plurality of the psyche we might be better talk of a drive to "completeness"—is visible as a "red thread" running through the narrative of the person's life. This thread is the journey of individuation. Many a time an analyst, psychotherapist, or counsellor is struck by the fact that the very thing that the patient or client would wish to avoid most, their Achilles heel, is that very thing that their life seems to propel them into. It is as if their own unconscious insists on finishing the unfinished business, and, since what is unfinished in their lives may well relate to feelings and experiences that they do not want to have or own, then it really does seem as if "life" takes them into those very areas that they most want to avoid.

Anything associated with the Self archetype will be experienced as numinous, having a larger than personal dimension. An image, symbol, idea, cause, or person can be experienced as of greater value than the merely personal, something or someone for whom one might dedicate one's life. Since the Self function includes, but is supraordinate to, the personal self or ego function, it is also collective, and is, in some measure, "public property". This is why the Self figure may appear in dreams as a king or a queen, a president or a prime minister, a film star, or other celebrity. The whole cult of celebrities has it roots in collective projections of the Self archetype. Indeed, the etymology of the word "celebrity" is from "celebrate", relating to the performance of a religious ceremony. Thus, we can speak of "celebrating" a friend's marriage, or of a priest "celebrating" the Mass. Much is made clear if we begin to see how these latter-day celebrities, the television personality, the film star, the lead singer of a band, or the sporting hero or heroine, receive and perhaps also take on the archetypal projections of the public. They are seen like the gods or goddesses of old, and are, thus, worshipped and envied, appeased and adored.

Sometimes, however, the Self archetype is encountered in its more transcendent aspect, as, for example, when it is experienced in a dream as a disembodied voice, but, in my exploration of love relationships, I am more interested in those manifestations of the Self archetype that reveal its more immanent, personal aspect. It is this aspect that can so easily be projected on to someone we love, and most especially when we "fall in love". There is, thus, an element of transcendence that seems inextricably woven into the experience of falling in love. In the past, the artist's beloved was often experienced as a gateway to the divine, as is Dante's Beatrice. In *Alone of all Her Sex: the Myth and Cult of the Virgin Mary*, the Jungian analyst Marina Warner describes the poet's great achievement: "It was Dante's unique genius that he was able to achieve a reconciliation of this eternal quarrel between the body and the soul in the sublime synthesis of divinity and humanity that is Beatrice" (Warner, 1976, p. 162).

If we look at the archetype of the Self from a developmental point of view, the parents are the first and crucial carriers of the Self figure for the infant, and Edinger (1972) has described this process in detail. By embodying the archetype of the Self in its various manifestations, the parents allow the child to project aspects of the archetype on to them and so to come into relationship to it. Over time, the developing child is able to take back this projection to some extent, and to relate to these elements as inner objective factors. When this process has succeeded sufficiently well, the archetype of the Self is beginning to be realized. We could say that it is humanized to some extent, fleshed out, "incarnated" for the child (in the theological narrative, this is roughly equivalent to the divine being experienced as immanent), and the ego is properly enriched by its relationship to the Self archetype as experienced in those and later projections. But when the parents have not sufficiently embodied the Self archetype, then the child will have a sense of it only as an abstract notion, as "something disincarnate" (in theological language, the divine is experienced as only transcendent); the ego, lacking a personal, living relationship to someone who acts as carrier for the Self figure, is, thereby, diminished. There will be a sense of depletion, and the child may grow up belittling itself: the ego may deny any continuity with the Self and feel only self-abasement. Conversely, the child may grow up compensating for this lack by becoming grandiose: the ego has arrogated to itself the prerogatives of the Self archetype and shows signs of omnipotence, omniscience, and so on. From this, it can be seen how close the problem is to issues of narcissism. Note how, in the myth of Narcissus, Narcissus's problem, as described by Schwarz-Salant (1982), was that he was unable properly to love another human being: he treated all his lovers cruelly. His punishment was to become a flower, to exist at the vegetative level where there is no social or sexual intercourse, but only a process of self-fertilization. We could say, in terms of our theme, that his problem was precisely an inability to fall in love!

I would like to suggest that falling in love might sometimes be a person's way of incarnating the archetype of the Self. It might possibly occur most intensely in those people who have both a strong yearning for the transcendent and a history of the Self archetype not having been sufficiently incarnated by the parents. In this case, there may be a kind of "unfinished business", wherein the immanent aspects of the archetype have yet to be projected and to be experienced through the medium of another person. Of course, many other factors can be projected at one and the same time and on to one and the same person: we have looked at the projection of the parents in Chapter One, and of the inner partner and of the personal shadow earlier in this chapter, and all of these elements may be fused together in the experience of falling in love. We shall explore this fact later, but for now let us look more specifically at the particular projection of the archetype of the Self.

The Self in projection

It is when aspects of the Self figure are projected on to the lover that love may be felt to be a particularly transcendent experience. There may be feelings of adoration and even of worship in the experience: there is an idealization of the beloved and the lover has feelings of being unworthy of being loved in return. Sometimes, it is the very fact that the love is unreciprocated, or felt to be so, that provokes precisely this feeling. At the same time, the lover will feel uplifted by the experience of loving the beloved: their very love, whether or not reciprocated, will, at least in the first flush of love, bring the ego into relationship with the Self archetype. This will be experienced as tremendously uplifting in the person's life.

His Dark Materials is a tale partly about the value and efficacy of human love. In this trilogy, the writer gives us a new Adam and Eve myth, a different story of human "salvation" (Pullman, 1995.). In the girl Lyra's world, a parallel universe to our own, everyone has a personal "daemon", a real creature that is at the same time also their non-human alter ego. A child's daemon can take on a variety of animal forms; only when a person becomes adult does their daemon take on a fixed form. Will, a boy from our world, discovers his own daemon in the course of the tale. Thus, we all have a daemon, but very few are able to recognize the fact. But, in all the worlds, vital energy is being leaked away and the cause for this is not known. The climax of the story centres on the very first expression of Will's and Lyra's love for each other when each touches the other's daemon. To touch another's daemon, in Lyra's world, is taboo. It is precisely at this point, a moment of utmost intimacy, that both daemons take on the future form that each will now inhabit. Thus, the two children discover that once the narrative of human love truly begins, the daemon, previously a fluid creature capable of all forms, incarnates fully. The Self archetype has taken form, and, in the story, it is this event which has the power to regenerate their worlds. Here, through human love and sexuality, in direct contrast to the Adam and Eve myth, the lovers find in each other an experience of the immanent Self, and it is that which renews life.

In practice, because the Inner Beloved partakes of the qualities of the Self, the union of the ego with the Inner Partner possesses a numinous quality. The union is like that of a mortal with an immortal, a god or goddess, and through that "marriage" the mortal partakes of eternity. The inner figure is the yearned-for Beloved who is also lover and who, could we but know it, reciprocates our love and who whispers in the words of every love poem: "I love you; I have loved you since the beginning of time; I will love you till the end of time."

One woman, Clarissa, was deeply attracted to a friend, Jane, who did not feel the same way about her. Despite the difficulties of the situation, for instance, the fact that she was longing for sexual closeness as well as the intimacy, Clarissa, none the less, felt that a friendship with Jane was of more value than breaking with her altogether. Others could not understand this, and encouraged Clarissa to leave her. Yet, there was something in Clarissa's feelings for Jane that came across as life-affirming. Clarissa had had a much earlier dream that her "lover" (a woman unfamiliar to her in real life) expressed the deepest love for her and told her that she had always loved her. The quality of the dream was very beautiful. This dream character is the Self figure. Later, Clarissa painted a picture of the Lover. It depicted Jane's face and head with its long curling hair like waves. Clarissa portrayed herself as a tiny figure caught in the tresses of her loved one as if drowning in a sea. The giantess figure is archetypal, and the figure as painted had elements of a sea goddess. At the same time, the image of the lover ensnared in the "hyacinth" tresses of the beloved is a common metaphor as, for example, in Persian love poetry. Here, the subsuming of self did not come across in the negative way one might expect. Over time, Clarissa was able to begin integrate valuable qualities of this friend and this would have gone some way towards helping her to experience her first truly reciprocal relationship with a woman. I have come across many similar examples of this in heterosexual love.

The benefits of using the teleological approach

What does Jung's approach add to our understanding of the phenomenon of falling in love and what can this narrative tell us about the benefits to be gleaned? Above all, the idea of individuation, that each person has a natural and instinctive drive to wholeness and to becoming who they uniquely are, can give us a whole new perspective on falling in love. In this way of thinking, the value of falling in love cannot be measured by its success alone. Obsessive love, infatuation, unrequited love, all these variants may help the person to individuate if they are able to use the experience and harness the intensity of the emotions as the energy which can transform fixed, defensive ways of seeing and being. It is the heat in the cooking that can turn base lead into gold. What matters here, above all, is not the kind of passionate love, but one's attitude towards it. If it is allowed to be a means towards individuation, then falling in love may well be the event for a particular person that helps them shift from living in a state of alienation to one of belonging.

But it must not be forgotten that working on our inner love story furthers love relationships in the outer world also. We have here a two-way relationship between the inner world and the outer, whereby the outer love relationship influences the inner one and the inner one the outer. Falling in love can be a stage in the blossoming of either one of these or both. But the teleological narrative also allows us to give value to two key processes in falling in love that can bring results of great benefit and which might otherwise be dismissed as being simply defensive. One is *idealization*, which we explored earlier, and which we can now re-evaluate in full. The other is what we might term the *refinement* of love, due to obstacles on its path. I avoid the term sublimation, because Freud's definition of the term involves a process that we would now recognize as defensive.

Idealism revisited

We have already explored how the idealization of the beloved can be a defence against ambivalence. The presence of an obvious idealization may provoke the lover's friends and family into trying to get them to see sense and to be able to see their beloved as human and flawed. They may want to protect the lover from too bitter a disappointment by "letting them down gently". Parents may be better aware than their offspring of how unsuitable a partner their child's beloved may be for them and try to show them that this is the case. This is an understandable enough reaction but, even if it were to work, and it is more likely to promote the opposite result, it is one which may not be taking into account the extraordinary value that even an unsuitable romance might have. Sometimes, as counsellors or psychotherapists, we may fall into this dynamic unconsciously, and use our psychotherapeutic tools, such as analysis and interpretation, to deconstruct the delusion. But this may be premature, or even destructive. In order to help clarify the issue, I would like to distinguish between three different types of idealization. It can be argued, with reason, that idealization is idealization whatever its outcome, but I would suggest that these three distinct contexts differ sufficiently to make it useful to use these three categories.

Three types of idealization

Primitive idealization

First, there is that form of idealization described by Freud and elaborated upon by Melanie Klein, which we explored in detail in Chapter One. It is a primary, pre-egoic defence entailing a splitting of the loved object so that those things that are experienced as good are kept separate and uncontaminated by those things in the beloved that are experienced as bad. However, it is important to bear in mind that although idealization is a primitive form of defence, it can, of course, be used by a person at any time in their lives. We can idealize our own political party, our country, our training institutions, our own particular set of beliefs, anything with which we identify strongly. One only has to look at the ferocity of those passions acted out after a big football match to see that idealization and splitting are alive and well. But, as we have seen, this form of idealization involves a regression to very early infancy, when splitting takes place. It also, therefore, harkens back, as Edinger (1972) has described, to a time when the parents are also experienced predominantly as archetypes and as carriers of the Self. Hence, even in the most primitive of idealizations of this type, there will be some projection of elements of the Self archetype and, therefore, some genuine aspects of transcendence. They will, however, in this instance, be only very partial. The main purpose of this defence is to protect the person from the difficulties of ambivalence.

Idealization serving realization

The second form of idealization is that process we have explored above, whereby numinous qualities of the Self archetype can be projected outside of oneself and, ideally, over time be (re)introjected, having now been fleshed out, elaborated, so to speak, by the relationship to the carrier of those qualities. The beloved may not even need to have those qualities to any great degree for the projection to be successful.

The idealization of the novel

The third type of idealization is one we have not explored before. This can occur when the subject has had not enough exposure to close relationships that are good enough in early childhood. Such a one may discover a quality in the love object that is, in fact, quite ordinary, but that at first seems too good to be true; it could be a quality as unexceptional as a readiness to consider them and their feelings or a refusal to abuse them. If the relationship continues over time, such behaviour will begin to be taken for granted in a positive sense. What at first is felt to be impossible, indeed hardly conceivable, becomes an imagined possibility for the lover. With time, this "imagined possibility" becomes realized. Simply being loved by another human being is then experienced as the fulfilment of what had seemed previously an impossible dream. The analyst or psychotherapist, for example, who simply listens attentively to the patient, who is willing to respect what they have to say, and is prepared to honour their feelings—all very ordinary qualities in any adequate therapist—can be felt to be so outside of the usual world of the client, especially if that was absent in childhood, that at first this treatment is seen as ideal: the therapist or analyst is experienced by the client as being the *only one in the world* who can give them this kind of love.

Loving another is, indeed, actually very close to seeing, respecting, and, therefore, understanding them. Receiving good-enough love is, thus, very close to being adequately seen, understood, and respected. But for someone who has had so little of this in their lives, the offer is experienced as little short of miraculous, and the analyst can at first be viewed as an almost divine figure giving unconditional love. Over time, as the client integrates this experience, they become better able to perceive when good-enough love is being offered by other people, such as friends, or current or potential partners. As the evidence for the very real possibility of such a love begins to convince, so the figure of the therapist or analyst can diminish in importance—not because, and this is important, not because what has been achieved ceases to be significant, but because what had previously been seen as impossible is now possible. One could say the miracle has now become a commonplace occurrence. This is, therefore, not quite the same move as described above, where the analyst needs to be de-idealized. It is not the case that the therapist cannot or does not give the kind of "love" needed, but, rather, that this ordinary love takes its place alongside newly-found other loves. At first, the patient will see the analyst as more than ordinarily human, and may well project the Self, as in our second type of idealization, but this is only a danger if the projection is not taken back when the time is right.

There is a little anecdote described in Charlotte Brontë's biographical novel, *Villette* (1853). The story mirrors closely Charlotte's own experience of studying and teaching in a boarding school in Brussels. The heroine, Lucy Snowe, has fallen asleep at her desk. A master at the school has noticed this and, as she sleeps, has placed a shawl beneath her head and arms and another around her to keep her warm. From this point onwards, the schoolmaster, who is both exacting and at times tyrannical, becomes an unlikely object of love. We know from Charlotte Brontë's letters how intense were her feelings for the married Monsieur Héger, the real-life model for her Monsieur Paul. She wrote him many letters (see Smith, 1995), but he was married and, after a while, replied to none of them. This caused Brontë acute distress. In *Villette*, to the orphaned and alone young woman, the simple gesture clearly was experienced as extraordinary. There is a real pathos that someone should find so slight a gesture of consideration so important, but, in her subsequent idealization of Monsieur Paul, it is not that Lucy was "making too much of this gesture": to her, it clearly *was* something entirely out of the ordinary. Yet, it is the sort of gesture any loving mother might do for a child. If a therapist or partner can help such a person discover love and begin to take it for granted in their lives, then they have helped them to achieve no mean feat.

Let me illustrate this with a dream that I think entirely encapsulates this idea. It is the dream of a woman, Helen, who was working with a male analyst with whom she had fallen in love. She had written down the dream and as it is so pertinent to our theme I have asked for permission to reproduce it in detail:

I must fetch a herb—saxifrage—from the top of the Alps. A man is cleaning or mending the windows of my family house. He is a kind of helper, protector figure. I ask him to get me the herb as I know he can do it and I can't. He goes to the top of the Alpine mountain and then I see the whole scene as if I am him. The herb has a strange shape: it has a central cluster of leaves with tiny clusters surrounding it like little circles around a large central circle. I, as the man, must dig up both the central cluster and each smaller cluster separately and then replant them in exactly the same way in the little pot that I had for the purpose.

When I have the herb I go to visit a second man. He's my lover. He's very impressed with my having being able to get hold of the saxifrage only the very next day after it was required. However, it occurs to me that it would be better if I could fetch it myself in person, rather than asking another to do it for me. I do so.

Then a new scene: as part of a training event, a group of us are left to romp in a meadow. It seems to be expected of us that we should allow ourselves to behave like children. I let myself get into it and roll around and romp in the meadow which has a sudden sharp slope to it. What at the beginning seems a bit phoney becomes very carefree and joyous. Then I notice that the Alpine herb, saxifrage, is growing at the top of the slope. It is everywhere and is now even clearly labelled!

She had looked up saxifrage as she did not know the plant, and found that it is indeed an alpine plant named from the Latin "saxum" = rock, plus "frangere" = break. This little herb found in such a rarefied atmosphere has a miraculous quality to it: it is a breaker of rocks.

This woman's dream describes the quest to find the mythical herb that is the bestower of immortality, which is present in so many legends: it is the soma of the gods, and the herb in the epic of Gilgamesh or the herb which is the alexipharmic of the alchemists. Helen is helped in this quest by her analyst, the "windowcleaner", who is at first the only one who can bring back this rarefied form of love, although it transpires that in some mysterious way it is she who is performing the task at the same time as he is. This theme of being helped and also of doing the work oneself is a very apt one for analysis.

That the herb of immortality has here to do with love is shown by the presence of the second male helper figure, the archetypal lover. The single specimen must be carefully uprooted and transplanted so that it can be carried back down the mountains to a place where it can grow, a place that is more accessible. The dreamer knows she must make the journey and do the task in person, that is, in full consciousness, for it to be truly valid, and she does so. But, for love to flourish freely, it would seem that a regression must take place: the playfulness of the child must be allowed. The act of rolling perhaps evokes falling "head over heels" in love. It is noteworthy and quite remarkable that it is *in this very act* that the dreamer comes across the herb now growing plentifully all over the meadow. Its nature is now so clear to her that there can be no mistaking it.

What the dream points to is many of our most important themes. First, that it might, at the beginning, sometimes need to be the analyst who constellates the quality of love within the analysand. Second, that having made the precarious and difficult struggle at an unconscious level to bring back the precious life-giving boon, the lover must repeat the journey to find it in full consciousness. Third, that for this to be possible, first a regression, so common in the experience of falling in love, is required. Again and again Jung writes of how regression serves a leap forward: it is a "reculer pour mieux sauter". Since individuation is a journey towards wholeness, it reveals the truth that "unless ye become as little children ye cannot enter the kingdom of heaven". Finally, having allowed herself to regress fully, we see that it is *in the very act of regression* that she finds the herb growing freely everywhere around her. Love, even true, life-affirming love, is not so very uncommon once one has learnt how to recognize it for what it is and admit to oneself a need for it. But the quest might, none the less, be an effortful task, a long, hard journey up the very highest of mountain peaks, one which cannot, in the last analysis, be left to another, but must be done for oneself in full consciousness.

Readers used to mandala symbolism will note the strange figuration of the herb itself: the circular clusters that grow in a circle around the central cluster. The whole must be broken up into its constituent parts, but each of those parts must be separately contained and transported from a rarefied aspect of the psyche (the alpine mountain) to be transplanted in a more accessible part of the psyche (the meadow). In the same way, the quality of love must be deconstructed and each fragment carefully contained for it to be transposed in its entirety to the world of the everyday.

Lest this itself sounds too idealized, let me explain in more detail how I see it. Love, even unconditional love, is actually very common. It is something that we are all capable of *at certain times*: we can give it to our clients, to our friends, to our children or partners *at certain times* when that which is most self-giving in us takes priority over the need for a response: not because at that moment we are trying to make it do so, sometimes it simply emerges (it grows "wild" in nature just like the saxifrage), but then, having emerged naturally, it needs to be carefully cultivated. At other times, we may need to experience a response to our love, or it may need to depend upon some condition being met. This, too, is only natural. I shall explore in Chapter Five the relationship between "need-love" and "gift-love", as both have been termed, but for now let us just acknowledge that adequate, "good enough" love will contain a mixture of conditional and unconditional love at different times.

Working through idealization

Dependant on what type of idealization has taken place will be the process needed to work it through. I have identified three different processes, each relating to the three different forms of idealization. These are *de-idealization, realization,* and *normalization.*

De-idealization

In the first kind of idealization, the primitive type that involves splitting as a defence, the love object needs to be exposed to a process of de-idealization or disillusion. This involves seeing the person as a "whole object", a feat akin to Klein's depressive position. In very primitive forms of idealization, this disillusion will take a correspondingly extreme form, that of disparagement. In order for the extremes of hyper-idealization and denigration to be integrated, an ability to contain ambivalence is required. The highly idealized figure who has been preserved as only good must now be seen as a mixture of both good and bad: and, indeed, all of us experience being loved best when we are loved with a "warts and all" kind of love. *All* falling in love will bring in some aspect of this defensive idealization, as the lover will experience some degree of regression to a childhood state of yearning for the undifferentiated wholeness of fusion with the mother.

Since it is defensive, this is the stage at which love is so often depicted as blind. If the lover cannot cope with seeing the shadow side of the other, then de-idealization proves to be too big a hurdle and complete disillusion sets in. Then aspects of the good object are irretrievable. This is the moment of "falling out" of love. "How could I have been so besotted with this person?" the disillusioned lover asks incredulously. The experiences of falling in love and falling out of love are both captured in the imagery of Shakespeare's play, *Midsummer Night's Dream*. The moment of de-idealization is symbolized by the point at which Oberon, King of the fairies, has Puck anoint an antidote to the eyes of his love-sick victims. In the case of his queen, Titania, she has been made to fall in love with Bottom wearing an Ass's head. When the antidote is applied she sees her former love object (so aptly named Bottom!) without the illusion of this kind of idealized love. He is, at that point seen to be, quite literally, an Ass! Oberon becomes a kind of Cupid/Eros figure who can play about with people's hearts and create or un-create happy endings, just as in life. But we must note, in passing, the misogynistic twist to the tale: Shakespeare has his Oberon character use the power of the juice to dominate his wife and win from her a love-object that was originally hers, the little page boy.

If this de-idealization is weathered (by both parties!) a good-enough relationship can be maintained. Person (1988) notes that the relationships that do best are those that are shown to maintain a certain amount of idealization, but, since the term suggests some-thing unreal and the selection of a significant other is entirely normal, I would prefer to call it something like preference: prefer-ence is the feeling state that confers the quality of specialness on the beloved. In reciprocal love, each is given the delightful sense of being special to someone who is special to oneself.

Realization (of elements of the Self)

With the second form of idealization, as mentioned above, what needs to happen is that the numinous qualities of the Self archetype are integrated, that is, re-introjected, having now been more fully fleshed out. In Freud's psychodynamic theory and in object relations theory, the term "introjected" is used because these elements are not seen as originally belonging to the subject. For Jung, however, they are elements of the objective, non-personal psyche that are rendered personal by coming into relationship with the ego. The better the relationship of the ego to the totality of the psyche, the more realized such qualities will be.

Normalization

With the third form of idealization, what needs to happen is that, having had an experience of love that *seems* ideal, because too good to be true, according to the lover's past experience, the subject goes on to have enough key experiences of love over time that can begin to be taken for granted in the positive sense. Such experiences, thus, become an imagined possibility for the future; no longer extraordinary, no longer too good to be true. This is the process described in the above dream, where the precious herb is found to grow everywhere.

However, there is perhaps a fourth form of idealization, connected to the others and yet distinct from them. This is to do with how the lover, in projecting the archetypal aspects of the Self on to the beloved, may yet, at the same time, be properly seeing the numinous in the other. It is a process I have come to call "resonance". It reveals an ability to see numinous qualities that are actually present in the other. This fact may account for the extremely positive effect a person's love may have on the loved one. If someone that we love and admire sees the best that is in us, and we experience that as precisely *seeing* that best, rather than projecting on to us something better than we are (which will make us feel unseen and uncomfortable, waiting for when disillusion inevitably sets in), then we might begin to feel that we can aspire to become what the other has glimpsed in us. This time it is the loved one who is given an imagined possibility.

This, I suggest, is what the Lebanese writer and poet, Kahlil Gibran, was referring to in a letter to his friend Mary Haskell (Hilu, 1972). He wrote: "The professors in the academy say, 'Do not make the model more beautiful than she is,' and my soul whispers, 'Oh, if you could only paint the model as beautiful as she really is'"

(Letter dated 8th November, 1908). The art academy teachers are warning the students not to flatter their subjects by exaggerating outward traits of beauty, but Gibran describes an inner seeing of an inner beauty.

To put it as clearly as possible in psychological terminology: when a person loves another in this way, the latter gets a sense of being seen as being more than just their personal ego: they are given a glimpse of the numinous within themselves, an experience of the Self, or, to put it in theological language, the spark of the divine. In this way, too, the Self can be realized for them. What has existed before only in potential is dreamed into being.

Of course, in practice, any or all of these components of idealization are likely to be found in combination. It can, however, be very useful to be able to sort out which component is which. Once this becomes clear, a person is better equipped to take back or not take back, as appropriate, what has been projected; to distinguish what is real and what is an illusion. What remains, as Jung wrote with such insight, serves kinship: our connection to others.

Love's refinement and the obstacles to love

However, we must bear in mind that a significant factor in some people's love stories is the part played by obstacles on the "path of true love". These obstacles may seem simply to denote pathology: a woman, for example, continues to love a man despite the fact that she is aware at some level that he is unable to commit himself in a relationship; a man cannot leave the woman who treats him with contempt, and so on. But, as we have seen above, the fact that the journey of individuation is unique to each person means that falling in love, as an important step on that journey, may be fulfilling different purposes for different people. We have seen how, in an ordinary reciprocal love affair, the ordinary companionate and sexual needs of the two people can be fulfilled, and, in such a case, falling in love has helped each on that part of their journey. But what about those instances where obstacles to love seem to be part and parcel of the love experience itself, and even intensify the love? This is not always the case, but when it is, the obstacles seem to fulfil an extremely important role in that they would seem to test the love itself and, in testing it, demand a degree of sacrifice. The sacrifice itself may then refine the love and, in the literal meaning of the word "sacrifice", make it in some way sacred. This very process can both ennoble the two lovers and the love itself. But we must note that this particular version of the love story is by no means the only one on the path to individuation through passionate love. Impediments can take a variety of forms and, therefore, fulfil a variety of purposes. For that reason, I shall outline a few main versions of these.

Outer obstacles to love

There are certain circumstances surrounding a love affair in which the physical/sexual expression of love must be ruled out, but where some form of closeness may be possible. In this case, the lovers may have a connection of some kind, if only in their feeling connection to each other, but cannot consummate their love. This could be called *celibate love*. (I use this term to distinguish it from "chaste love", which can include non-illicit sexual expressions of love, that is, chaste sex can be used to describe the sex between married couples.) There are other circumstances where sexual expression is not barred, but where the ordinary bonding process of a life led together is not possible. The lovers may consummate their love, but they have to remain separate in some other way. We can call this *attenuated love*. And last, we have *unreciprocated love*, where the lover loves a beloved without being loved by him or her in return. We can explore each of these constraints in turn

Chaste love

A constraint on the sexual expression of love may apply when two people love each other but there are obstacles to its consummation. These might be in terms of duty and/or one's own conscience: the films *Casablanca* and *Brief Encounter* describe situations where both duty and conscience would have stood in the way. Considerations of marriage commitments or children can cause two lovers to rule out sexual relations. There may also be some other more unusual constraint, such as a religious calling to celibacy. Mythically, we have the constraint of a kind of miscegenation: in *Les Sylphides*, the Prince may not touch the wings of the fairy that he loves or she will die. This theme of touch being tabooed is evidenced in a spate of films that have a vampire hero or heroine being unable to touch the person they love. These stories, well told, seem never to fail to spark off a degree of longing in many among their audiences or readers. This sort of situation is ripe for the experience of a soul connection. The bar to any sexual form of relationship will create an emphasis on the quality of kindred spirit, and I suggest it is this soul quality which so stirs us.

In such relationships, the longed for sexual union may take on the aspect of an idealized goal in a couple who are spiritually inclined. The desire to possess and be possessed by the beloved may take on the quality of a mystical union. Oddly enough, should sexual expression become possible at a later date, then the fact of this goal being realized may mean that it can no longer carry the projection of something as ideal as union with the Self, the "inner divinity", and then the loved one may take on a much more human dimension for each lover. For this reason, the lovers sometimes choose themselves to eschew a sexual expression of their love.

Attenuated love

This second instance is a love relationship where the two people have had a sexual relationship but cannot be close to each other geographically, or cannot have prolonged time together. This is the story of all the classical love tragedies, such as *Romeo and Juliet*, *Tristan and Iseult*, and so on. A good and more recent example of this is given in the film, *The Bridges of Madison County*, made in 1995 and adapted from the novel by Robert Waller. The film tells the story of Francesca, a loving but lonely wife and mother, who has a brief affair with a visiting photographer, Kincaid, while her family are away. She is transformed by the experience in a process that we can only call individuation. That transformation is beautifully depicted by the actress Meryl Streep. Yet, for all the extraordinary blossoming of self that occurs with the love affair, Francesca chooses to stay loyal to her marriage. She recognizes that predictability can stifle this kind of love; she knows that her husband and her children need her, and she tells Kincaid that if she left her family she would become something other than the woman he loved. Yet, her last wish to have her ashes scattered over the bridges of the title symbolizes that, with Kincaid, she had a closeness of "soul" if not of geographical proximity.

Often, in such relationships, it is the absence of predictability, the mundane "over the toast and marmalade" experience, which may serve to maintain idealization. Each lover is thus allowed to avoid encounter with the other's shadow, and this allows for projections of the Self to be maintained. In this case, it is not the *sexual union* with the other that is seen as holding all that one most longs for, but the *everyday closeness* to him or her. The lovers long for a place, a paradise, where they can be together all the time. And, as long as distance must be maintained, everyday closeness will most likely continue to carry the projection of closeness to the Self. This may mean that the Self archetype remains a disincarnate entity, evoked only by the longed-for paradise. It is likely to remain unrealized until such time as the lovers can experience projection again, either by becoming closer or by falling in love with a new love object. Those who fall in love in such circumstances may fall in love again and again, until such time as they are able to form a long-term relationship and/or work through the projections of the Self. We shall look in more detail at that process a little later.

It is the obstacle to closeness, here, whether caused by having only limited time or limited space with each other, which serves to make the love more attenuated. Love is refined by the very fact that it cannot be acted upon. John Donne (1635) in his poem, "A Valediction: Forbidding Mourning", has the lovely image of beaten gold for the way in which distance refines love. The poet is about to depart, but forbids his love to grieve, telling her that theirs is a different kind of love from the mundane:

> Our two souls therefore, which are one,
> Though I must go, endure not yet
> A breach, but an expansion,
> Like gold to aery thinness beat. (p. 84)

It is as if distance itself stretches out the love, thereby refining it. Gold, the currency of that era, is beaten into gold leaf for its use in fine art, a detail that will be no accident in Donne's use of the image. There is a transformation of the quality of love in this process.

In Philip Pullman's trilogy, the fact that the two lovers, Lyra and Will, are doomed never to be able to be together, but can only have the most tenuous form of connection across two different virtual worlds, two different dimensions in space, if not in time, adds a quality of the numinous and the eternal to their love. In so many classical tales of tragic love of this kind the lovers are only united in death. But it is this very fact of union in death—the lovers sometimes are actually buried together, as are Romeo and Juliet in Shakespeare's play—that points to the eternal or supra-mundane quality to their love.

The situation where love is reciprocated, but where the loved one is, for some reason, ineligible, can repeat itself as a pattern in a person's life. In a psychotherapeutic practice, one may notice in certain clients a tendency to fall in love with ineligible but loving love objects. This may reveal an unconscious fear of intimacy on both sides. Transference love for the analyst or therapist is often an instance of this, but here the intimacy of the therapeutic work can allow what is being defended against to emerge. We saw above that, in all but the most delusional of transferences, there is often some degree of affinity between therapist and patient and this remains when all the projections are withdrawn.

Unreciprocated love

Repeating patterns of unreciprocated love affairs show more clearly a dynamic of unreciprocated parental relationships: the first "love affair" is with the mother or primary carer(s), and if this love is unreciprocated for the child, for whatever reason (a depressed or anxious mother, for example), then this can set the pattern for all later loves. Yet, even here, the love object can take on significance as a carrier of the Self archetype. This probably relates, as we saw earlier, to what Edinger (1972) highlights in the early fusion for the infant of the parents with this archetype. Thus, while falling in love with someone who does not return our love would seem to be a problem of fate in our outer world, it is often a reflection of the state of things within as described below.

Inner obstacles to love

Sometimes, one can clearly see the pathology that prevents the yearning for the ideal from being fleshed out in an ordinary human love. One has the feeling with clients that this kind of love presents a form of defence. This is most clear when there is no clear external obstacle for keeping the love as a distant one. In Ishiguro's novel, *Remains of the Day* (1988), from which the 1993 film was made, Stevens, the butler, cannot allow himself to experience his own love for Miss Kenton, the housekeeper. In the book the narrator justifies this avoidance but it, none the less, strikes a psychologically-minded reader as being defensive: a possibility of making the ideal real is being avoided. This is an inner psychological obstacle: it is sublimation, and, as such, is a defence. In this defence, needs at the more instinctual level are transmuted to a more rarefied level. The reverse, concretization, is meeting needs for something sublime at a more concrete level. Either way, the need is not being met *at the appropriate level*, but is being substituted for and remains essentially repressed.

In other instances, it strikes one that the person, in not finding an outer lover, is (unconsciously) keeping alive a yearning for the numinous that is actually served by the obstacles that prevent them living out the relationship in a more ordinary way. It is, then, as if it is the *inner relationship* that is unreciprocated, and it may be that this inner problem must first be addressed. If our *inner* love story has a beloved who is not free or eligible for love's consummation, then the obstacles within have to be removed at some point. In one's dreams—in one's inner world—no previous marriage of self or of the beloved, no vow, no taboo, no threat or danger, or insurmountable obstacle can ultimately stand in the way of this sacred union. All the obstacles—no matter how impossible—must be overcome. One man, Peter, who chose to stay faithful to his wife when he fell in love with another woman, dreamed years later about an unknown woman that he truly loved but who could not be his since *she* was married. The dream has given him an entirely different scenario from the original, real life one. Once he realized that this figure represented a contrasexual part of himself that must be integrated, Peter discovered, to his surprise, that a second dream presented its own solution to the conflict: the woman's husband leaves the couple together! It is the shadow, here the dream-woman's husband, who must let go of the Inner Beloved, because she really belongs with the dreamer, and the union is with him.

Transference as projections of aspects of the Self

Transference, of course, is a special case of projection. It is projection in the analytic setting. Freud used the term because he became aware of how frequently it occurred in analysis and he discovered its therapeutic value. By projecting internal objects on to the analyst, the patient can make these projections conscious, and so have the possibility of integrating them. It is now used by extension for the same process in other types of therapeutic relationship.

I would like to make a case for extending the usage of the term in order to highlight more clearly why it is that an analyst or therapist (originally the doctor) is so often the hook for projections. Using a Jungian perspective, I suggest it would be helpful to use the term transference for any projection upon an individual whose *role* has a distinctly archetypal quality to it. I am not, here, referring to the *content* of the projection: that will always have some archetypal dimension, for example, when a person projects their mother imago on to another, that projection will contain elements that derive from the personal mother of the projector and elements that belong to the archetype of the Mother. I am suggesting using the term transference when it is *the role itself* that has the archetypal associations with it. In other words, *the role carries prestige*. Thus, roles such as analyst, therapist, counsellor, doctor, nurse, and so on relate to the archetype of the *Healer* and carry the prestige associated with that archetype. Then we have roles such as teacher, tutor, mentor, coach, and so on, which relate to the archetype of the *Teacher*. There are the roles of priest, minister, shaman, spiritual leader, guru, and, again, analyst or therapist, and so on, which relate to the archetype of the *Priest*, the mediator between the human and the divine worlds. Then there are those public figures who belong to the collective and who have some particular prestige by virtue of their public role, such as royalty, a president, a celebrity, and so on. These roles make very good hooks for projections of the Self, and such a role could be termed the *Luminary*.

Jungians use the term "archetypal transference", but, with this term, the emphasis is on the content of the projection (archetypal material). Why I think it is worth having this broader usage of the term "transference", as I have defined it, above, is that the emphasis is on the role. The more universal the role, the bigger is its prestige. The prestige is shored up by the particular traditions of the society, culture, or subculture within which the role has its sociological context. Hence, the prestigious person will always occupy a "larger-than-life" dimension for the person projecting, and this has particular consequences for that relationship. Thus, the Hindu traditions assign a particular significance to the Guru, the Catholic tradition to the Spiritual Director, and so on. For someone entirely outside of those traditions, the transference on to these specific figures is not likely to happen and may well be a complete mystery to them.

Thus, transference is here defined as that special case of projection in which the intensity of feeling is evoked by virtue of the prestigious, that is, "Self-like", role played by the other. Of course, it is important to bear in mind that every human relationship will contain projections: we never see a person absolutely clearly without putting on to them some element that resides within our own psyches. But relationships of love or antagonism always reveal instances of particularly strong projection. The clue to the existence of a projection lies in the very intensity of the feeling. In passionate love, it is the presence of projection, where the internal image is superimposed on the perceived figure and obscures accurate perception of the real person, which is behind the idea that love is blind. Yet, we intuit that love should be clear-sighted: we desire to be loved "warts and all", seen and understood for what we are and exactly as we are.

My wider definition of transference can help us to understand a little better what processes may be going on when a person falls in love with someone who has a prestigious role. This is why a woman might so readily fall in love with her fitness coach, a parishioner with the priest, a man for a screen goddess, and so on. It may be that, in youth, we are more likely to fall for those with evident power or beauty, that is, those who might unconsciously be perceived as being a good mate, while in the latter part of life we might be more likely to fall in love with someone who holds "spiritual" qualities: a figure who is a mentor, a muse, or a soul-mate. If, in youth, love has much to do with the finding of a mate and a suitable partner for one's future progeny, what is its purpose in later years, when these functions have been fulfilled? Perhaps it can be a discovery of the numinous both within another and within oneself.

All that I have been describing here is one particular aspect of passionate love: it relates to a love that is not able to attain the fulfilment of its most natural desires. That type of passionate love in which the natural desires come to be fulfilled is, of course, just as valid and, I would suggest, may deserve the name of love just as much as the more ordinary kind, but it is not celebrated so much in film, literature, and myth. The humdrum love for a spouse, for example, might contain as many noble feelings as thwarted love. After all, self-sacrifice can be found in either form. If that is the case, then what is it about the first that seems to create such a good hook for projections of the Self? I would suggest that it is some aspect of longing. The yearning for love which has some kind of obstacle to its fulfilment draws a person beyond themselves: it is the hunger rather than the feast, and that hunger for some missing element which lies within becomes the motivation for individuation through the development of one's inner world.

The dangers

The fact that falling in love may be a path to individuation is fraught with danger. There is a danger of thinking that one makes this journey in isolation. Some people misinterpret Jung and think that individuation is associated only with the inner world, implying isolation from others. Jung's work is often wrongly used because of this. Pickering (2008) rightly cautions against using the other as a ladder for one's own development, and aptly describes how this attitude might play itself out in couple relationships:

> I meet Jo who has qualities I need to develop. I represent qualities he needs to develop. We find ourselves in conflict because this makes us both confront our respective developmental deficits that we would rather not face. We dutifully trot off to couple therapy and work on these respective areas in ourselves. The real lover becomes superfluous and expendable, just as in Plato's theory.

> If we are relational and interdependent beings, then the felt tension between the individuation [meant in Mahler's (1975) sense rather than in Jung's sense] needs of the individual and the requirements of the relationship is a false dichotomy. [p. 102]

In other words, an individual person has relationship needs and is, therefore, fulfilling important personal needs through re-lating. Jung similarly does justice to this point in his definition of individuation. I would disagree with Pickering, however, by maintaining that the fact that a lover may make all sorts of projections, whether archetypal or purely personal, which arise willy-nilly and threaten to blot out the face of the beloved, does not necessarily imply narcissism. We cannot stop this process: it will happen with or without our consent and, as we have seen, has the great value of helping us to grow. As I have said before, it is the person's attitude that is paramount. It is also a question of knowing *when* to take a projection back: timing is all.

All of this is a fractional process. How it can work positively in practice is something like this: I fall in love with another and the intensity of the experience provokes an amalgam of desire and dread, hope and fear, longing and vulnerability. So much is at stake, so many feelings evoked, that the beloved becomes the carrier of a rich panoply of projections, both personal and archetypal. But I love the other, and those projections obscure my vision of him or her. Not seeing my lover clearly creates disturbances in the relationship, and these distress me. The distress and the love I have for him or her may provide sufficient motivation for me to take back my projections. In taking these back, I am given back something of myself; in being given back myself, I feel grateful. In my gratitude, I feel beholden to my beloved and love him or her even more. In loving more, I project more, and so on. In a long-term committed relationship, while the "in love" feelings might diminish, there is the opportunity to get to know better both my loved one and myself.

There is a vicious circle that may arise in a similar way: I project on to my beloved as before, but the fact that the beloved is not like my projections becomes a source of irritation or disappointment. I am either unable or unwilling to work these through. Repeated irritations or disillusions may compound earlier experiences and I may be unable to let go of my familiar constructs. New imagined hurts, such as betrayal or abandonment, re-traumatize old ones, and I become more and more closed off and defensive. Pickering (2008), a couple therapist herself, describes this accurately. It takes much forgiveness to allow another to be different from our projections.

Drawing on Jung's typology, Jung (1921), I would suggest that an extrovert, more prone to fulfilling the need for love in outer relationships, might well need their journey in love to take them into their inner world for once, and may, indeed, find that circumstances conspire to make this happen, while an introvert, more prone to living out and fulfilling those needs within their internal world, might well need their journey in love to take them into relationships with others, and may also find that circumstances conspire to make this happen. What can too hastily be called "acting out" might actually be, for an introvert, a vital and necessary process of realization, an incarnation of something that has hitherto remained only in the archetypal realm. Jung himself, being an introvert, clearly saw the dangers of trying to make the whole thing only an internal event. This defence we could call "acting in", while Freud, an extrovert, saw clearly the dangers of "acting out". Jung pointed out that it is often through the shadow function, the opposite one to our preferred function, that individuation might arise.

Another danger is to do with the fact that we are dealing with archetypes. Since what is archetypal is, by definition, something held in common by all human beings, it is very easy to lose sight of the diversity expressed in individual human beings, of the differences found in different cultures, in the different sexes, in the different sexual orientations, in different races and ethnic groups, and so on. Archetypal theory, valuable as it is, will fail, and fail miserably, unless it is continually brought in line with the most recent discoveries in anthropology, in sociology, in the sciences. We must critique approaches that merely reflect the dominant culture and must include the perspectives of diverse groups, especially those whose voice is not so readily heard. It is a great shame that too many Jungians use archetypal theory as a way of digging in their heels when challenged by diversity. Because Jung himself had aimed at a model that does, indeed, take into account the psychological type and projections of the model-maker (even though he does not always succeed in this), it is too much of a temptation to be lazy in our thinking and imagine that this opus is complete. Such a work is never complete.

The danger, mentioned above, of seeing individuation as a purely personal or exclusively psychological journey, is counterbalanced by the narratives of the major religions and of the myths that explore the nature of love. It is to examples of these that we shall now turn.

CHAPTER FIVE

The religious discourse

I am going to explore five particular accounts of Eros that could be grouped together under what might broadly be termed the religious narrative in order to see what each adds to our understanding of passionate love. The first account is in C. S. Lewis's work, *The Four Loves* (1960); the second in mythology, using two tales, Tristan and Iseult and Eros and Psyche, and last, the account given by two religious teachers, the Sufi poet, Rumi, and a Hindu Vedic scholar, Shastri.

Although our subject is falling in love, I will not explore that aspect of mystical love that is specifically a "falling in love" with the Divine. In religious traditions, such a form of love is directed at a transcendent (rather than immanent) God; in other words, the "Other" in this version is a transcendent being. Whether, in Hinduism, it is expressed in the love poems of Meera, who sings to a divine Krishna, or those of John of the Cross, who bases his love songs on the biblical *Song of Songs*, the loved one is a non-incarnate aspect of God who, if anything, is seen as a lover or husband who wishes the beloved to have no other loves. The Jungian analyst, Dourley (1987) has written with much insight as to how the split between the divine and the human can be healed through the journey within the psyche. By contrast we will explore certain accounts within the above religious traditions which explicitly refer to passionate love between two people. We can see that much of the writing about Eros, as it is termed drawing on classical Greek tradition, adopts a polarized idea of love as being essentially either "selfish" or "unselfish". In this polarization we can detect the struggle between the rebellious id and an overly developed super ego, both continually at war with each other. When this is too polarized duty and desire are experienced as worlds apart. This split can be mirrored in an individual who makes a corresponding split between love for another human being and love for the divine.

The Four Loves

In his little book, Lewis (1960) gives a detailed description of the nature of four kinds of love: affection, friendship, Eros, and charity. For our purposes, it is his chapter on Eros that is relevant. As a religious philosopher, Lewis is specifically interested in the journey to God. Treated from a purely psychological viewpoint, we can talk of this journey as one of the ego towards the Self. For a more in-depth study of this journey, I refer the reader to Edinger (1972). I am not, here, equating "God" and "the Self". "God" is a theological term and, as such, remains outside of the scope of psychology, but psychology must account for the God *image* within the psyche.

Lewis writes, "By Eros I mean of course that state which we call 'being in love'" (p. 87). This is not the same as sexuality, in that sexual love can occur without Eros and Eros contains many other things besides sexual activity. Eros, thus, is "a uniquely human variation" of sexuality that develops within love. With great common sense, he notes that it is not whether the act of making love is "pure" Eros or simple lust that brings morality into the picture, but, rather, such things as "the keeping or breaking of promises", justice or injustice, charity or selfishness.

But when Lewis goes on to describe certain inadequacies of Eros, to my mind he writes too much like a confirmed bachelor. For example, he takes marriage as a distraction from "waiting uninterruptedly on God" (p. 92): all those "practical and prudential cares" within a marriage, the "multiple distractions of domesticity" that get in the way.

But this is tantamount to saying that marriage cannot *of itself* be a journey to individuation, and this is patently not the case. If that were so, the majority of the human race would be having difficulty individuating! Guggenbühl-Craig (1977) makes a really good case for a contrary position, seeing a committed relationship as a path of individuation. To put that into the religious language that Lewis himself might use, marriage can be a path to salvation. If he sees the practical cares of a long-term committed relationship as only a distraction from waiting on God, rather than a possible means of serving him, then it is no wonder that, for Lewis, falling in love—a possible step on the way—will be likewise suspect.

Another point that I would like to contest is his view that while Eros can perhaps give us an experience of god-likeness, it cannot really be of help in a journey towards God. Again, I will make no comment on religious belief, but simply look at this idea psychologically in terms of the ego's nearness to the Self, here, the god-image within the psyche. Lewis describes (p. 4) two kinds of "nearness" to God, one is *likeness to God*: we are made in God's image and this is a given of human nature; the other is *nearness of approach*: the human being is "nearest" to God in those states in which "he is most surely and swiftly approaching his final union with God, vision of God and enjoyment of God" (*ibid*.). The two, he writes, are not the same thing. To illustrate what he means by each of these terms he gives us an analogy (pp. 4–5). He envisages a circular mountain walk. We have set off from a village, which is our home and are now returning. At mid-day, we come to a cliff-top, and from there can see our village directly below us. However, to reach it we must take a very circuitous route. The cliff-top is nearness-by-likeness; the long route down, nearness-of-approach. Later he goes on thus to write,

> We must not give unconditional obedience to the voice of Eros when he speaks most like a god. Neither must we ignore or attempt to deny the god-like quality. This love is really and truly like Love Himself. In it there is real nearness to God (by Resemblance); but not, therefore and necessarily, a nearness of Approach. [p. 104]

In other words, passionate love has a divine quality that is properly like God, but which does not get us any nearer to God. Lewis does allow that this "nearness of likeness" can become a "nearness of approach", but only as a *paradigm* or *example* "built into our natures" of the love we should have for God and others (p. 105). In other words, it cannot lead there of itself. Later (p. 109), he does fleetingly allude to how Eros may be a preparation for loving others as we love ourselves, but he does not give any detail as to how this may come about. He merely mentions that it is up to us to keep the vows Eros has impelled us to make and that in marriage we have to "take the rough with the smooth". Couples are helped in this endeavour by the Christian virtues. From this, it would seem that his focus is specifically on marital fidelity. Lewis sees the problem of Eros essentially as posited in the conflict between Eros in adultery and fidelity in marriage. I would rather argue not that it is simply the presence of Eros in itself that brings value to the lovers, but, rather, what they make of it. We can stumble across love like some untutored Parsifal who, in his innocence, stumbled upon the Holy Grail at the very beginning of his quest but could not claim it (then) because he did not ask whom it served nor to what place it was being taken. He failed to discover its meaning at that moment.

Lewis does not have a model for how Eros could be transcendent of itself, or help to transform a person for the good. Perhaps one misleading feature of his analogy of the route back down from the mountain to one's home village is that it presupposes we actually *know* the way home: in truth, although we may have intimations of how to reach psychological wholeness or the Self, it is a path without a detailed map. General directions might be given in scriptures or other wisdom traditions, but, as Jung asserted, the path for each individual must be unique to them; this is the crux of his notion of individuation. Perhaps a better analogy for the process, then, would be a climb *up* the mountain, during which we are occasionally given a glimpse of the lovely peak soaring miles above us. That glimpse might be more than just a paradigm or an example: it might be one of the best ways for some (the mountain climber, for example) of being able to tell whether or not they are going in the right direction! True, seeing how far one is from the summit could cause a person to lose heart and to give up, but it could also, depending on the individual's attitude, inspire them to further endeavour! Lewis seems not to consider that discovering what may be termed the "divine" element within might, of itself, especially if repeated often, transform the individual.

Interestingly enough, Bowlby (1980) cites Lewis's journal, *A Grief Observed*, in which the writer described his personal experiences after his wife's death. Bowlby notes how, in two passages, Lewis, while a deeply religious man, describes how one seems not to experience comfort from God when desperate, but only when happy. Bowlby explores Lewis's own account of his mother's death when he was only nine, and of how his father

> always temperamental, became so distraught that he was in no state to comfort his grieving sons. On the contrary, he alienated them: "he spoke wildly and acted unjustly ... With my mother's death all settled happiness, all that was tranquil and reliable, disappeared from my life". [Bowlby, 1980, p. 241]

Bowlby suggests here that Lewis would have formed defences of avoidant attachment from that time, resulting in a large degree of inhibition of feelings and growing up to be "intensely introspective". Does this go some way towards explaining why Eros, the love to be found in intimate relationships, seems to Lewis to be an inferior form of love to caritas or agape? Can ordinary needs for human love and companionship, comfort, and assurance, get displaced onto God? And is this what Lewis is doing? If so, not only would this create a conflict between human love and divine love as if the two are in competition with each other, but it would also create a split in one's experience of love for God, as if God's attitude was to dismiss neediness and dependence. If patterns of avoidant attachment lead us to believe that our neediness, dependence, or longing for connection with another is suspect in some way, then it is not hard to see how this belief might be ascribed to the Divine.

It is perhaps from this piece of personal history that Lewis makes a distinction between need-love and gift-love that keeps the two mutually exclusive. Although he makes a very good case for the blessings of receiving without shame, Lewis keeps the acts of giving and receiving distinct in a way that does not always hold. In the process of individuation, as the ego is more and more subsumed into the Self, the distinction between who gives and who receives, lover or beloved, becomes less clear. If a person genuinely delights in giving to others (and studies of happiness show that everyone needs a degree of giving to others in their life in order to be happy), then they will readily admit to an experience of joy in being allowed to "indulge" that need. Aristotle (1953) puts it beautifully in his valuation of friendship. He writes (VIII: 5),

> And to love one's friend is to love one's own good. For the good man by the very act of becoming friends of the other becomes that other's good ... It may therefore be said that each of the friends loves his own good and makes the balance equal by wishing the good of the other and pleasing him. [p. 237].

Lewis does concede of Eros that one of the first things that it does is "to obliterate the distinction between giving and receiving" (p. 91), yet he does not make anything more of this insight.

Last, Lewis sees in the act of sex a "Pagan sacrament", by which he means that the individual man and woman enact something universal: "In us all the masculinity and femininity of the world ... are momentarily focused" (p. 98). He is, of course, describing what Jung would call archetypal. Yet, he makes the mistake of seeing mastery as the archetype of the masculine and subjugation as the archetype of the feminine. In other words he is describing complexes rather than archetypes. Because Lewis's God is implicitly male, indeed "more masculine than the male", and because for him there is no equivalent divine feminine, then the "pagan sacrament" behind the sexual act can take only that form in which the man enacts the Sky Father and the woman the Earth Mother, "a god and goddess between whom there is no equality" (p. 99). But what, we might ask ourselves, of Innana, Queen of heaven, who takes Dumuzi the shepherd as her consort? Why cannot this divinely feminine condescension also be available to enact? I suppose the answer is that, to Lewis, a traditional Christian, this enactment can only be Pagan. And, for him, the Christian version of marriage is one in which the husband is head over his wife "as Christ is to the Church". We can note in passing that this literal reading of St Paul's analogy arises when biblical readings are not recontextualized.

Lewis rationalizes the "head of the household" theme by claiming that the crown of this headship, being like that of Christ, is the crown of crucifixion, a crown of self-giving. He writes, "The sternest feminist need not grudge my sex the crown offered to it either in the Pagan or in the Christian mystery. For the one is of paper and the other of thorns" (p. 101). That is the same thing as to console nineteenth century woman over the lack of franchise by saying that having the vote is a burdensome responsibility and one that she is far better off without! Lewis's argument runs that self-giving is suffering, and it is a husband's duty to protect his wife from (this particular form of) suffering in their marriage. But self-giving, as we have said, is not all suffering, and even if it were, as Lewis suggests, a noble suffering, why should a spouse want to protect their partner from it? Surely, to share something so noble would be for him an example of the Christian ideal of charity? Furthermore, it is clear that, for Lewis, the self-giving he intends here is of the particular kind which involves forbearance, forgiveness, and care, that is, patronage, but most certainly not the kind which would concede a woman her sovereignty, her right as an individual to make her own choices and decisions. By contrast, see Young-Eisendrath (1999).

We may note in passing that the Judeo-Christian tradition has, in fact, a beautiful antidote to this lack of reciprocity in the "Song of Songs". It is perhaps one of the most unlikely of books to have been retained in the Christian or even the Jewish canon. Nowhere does it explicitly mention God, the idea that it describes the relationship of a people or a person with God is an interpretation, and nowhere in the text is there a clear indication that the text must be interpreted in this way. The song seems to have been preserved as such mostly because it is a piece of transcendent beauty, also perhaps because something convinces the reader that it is at heart a religious poem. It describes a love that is frankly erotic, and yet also entirely mutual, where lover and beloved both give and receive love, where each would seem to be equal and where each is loved as they love and loves as they are loved.

And last, to return to Lewis, he rightly points out the dangers of Eros's claim of a divine (absolute) authority as such, and of it thus being permitted to override ordinary obligations. These dangers relate to the danger of inflation as described by Jung. Lewis sees this as a problem relating only to the "natural" loves and not to love of God. However, in an age where we are acutely aware of how distorted religious beliefs can be used to justify negative deeds such as violence or coercion (as is clear in any religiously motivated terrorism), we can see that the criterion of self-giving is not an entirely fool-proof one. After all, efforts at religious conversion, even coercive ones, may be seen by its advocates as gift-love. A clear example of this was seen in the Christian crusaders, who quite genuinely believed that to force another into religious conversion, even by the sword, was to care for what was most valuable in them (their immortal soul) rather than for what was of relatively little value (their physical life). And Lewis's own description of the forbearing husband who tolerates a wife whom he makes subordinate to him will impress very few modern women (and not many modern men) as an example of real generosity!

Must we polarize desire and duty, self-love and altruistic love in quite this way? Is God simply an object of love to compete with our other loves? Or could there be some way in which God can be seen as participating in those loves? Johnson (1983) takes up the myth of Tristan and Iseult, a medieval tale set in the time of King Arthur, and, using Jung's idea of the Animus and Anima, describes a new way out of the conflict. It is an interpretation that he calls Jungian, but I shall argue that this solution creates its own forms of dualism and, therefore, goes in a rather different direction from that which Jung intends. Jung, especially in his later writings, reached for non-dualistic ways of understanding the human psyche.

Tristan and Iseult

The story tells how Tristan, nephew to King Mark of Cornwall, has been sent by his uncle to bring back Iseult of Ireland to be Mark's Queen. But Tristan and Iseult become the victims of a love potion and fall in love. The tale is the tragic story of how, despite repeated attempts, neither is able to give the other up for the sake of fealty to their king. Finally, Tristan is undone by trickery, and only in death are the lovers united.

Drawing on de Rougemont (1956), whom he cites, Johnson (1983) notes that

> our modern Western society is the only culture in history that has experienced romantic love as a mass phenomenon. We are the only society that makes romance the basis of our marriages and love relationships and the cultural ideal of "true love". [p. xii]

He concludes, with de Rougemont, that, since love passion in the west is romantic and so often, as in our tale, adulterous, the solution (for the man) must be not to project the anima but to find her within. "If we . . . try to make her into a physical being by projecting her onto an external person, then we lose her sacredness" (*ibid.*, p. 170). For Johnson, therefore, the error is to have displaced religion from where it dwells within the psyche to outside of the psyche. Then:

> we have mixed our spiritual aspiration—our urge toward the divine—with our human relationships. This is the secret knowledge that is hidden behind the mystery of romantic love: how to live with and honor both of these powerful energies, which we have mixed together so deliciously and yet so dangerously in the wine of love. [*ibid.*, p. 61]

But this is to presuppose that religion belongs only within, and that spiritual aspiration and human relationships are not merely distinguishable but do not overlap. It is also to see projections merely as obfuscation of reality and not to see also their possibility of realizing—that is, making conscious and giving psychological life to—hidden aspects of the self. The role of the "mating archetype" is an archetype, and, as such, it is also numinous and will take us into relationship with others.

In so far as the tragic tale of Tristan and Iseult describes a real life situation, then Johnson is right to suggest that the lovers are forced by that situation to turn each within him- or herself. If, in our outer life, we love someone, and yet our own conscience (not necessarily the same as the superego, as I shall explore later) forbids us to consummate this love, then this fact is a very strong indication that it is the elements of our inner story that must be worked on. The Self might seem to call us into love while at the same time, in this case, forbidding sexual or other forms of expression of this love. But, as we have seen, as a myth that describes the story at the *inner* level, a myth of individuation, it *must* have a happy ending: the lovers must be allowed to come together whatever their loyalty and commitment to the King. If a male client or patient were to tell me a dream which told such a story within, where his beloved was married to another, then I might note that, at some level, the man's

Anima is fused with his shadow and needs to be freed in order for the two lovers to be able to unite. Remember the tale of the hunter who loses his Swan maiden wife to her other world for ever, and the other tale. which tells of how the hunter did not rest content with the loss of his Swan-maiden wife and laboured to win her back from her father-King. We saw how the first version of the tale tells of an as yet incomplete journey of individuation.

Johnson's treatment of the story of Tristan and Iseult does justice to its great beauty, but his conclusions are ultimately dualistic: they reveal a form of Platonic dualism prevalent in many Jungian writers, but, I suggest, not in Jung. For example, Johnson concludes:

> So much of our lives is spent in a longing and a search—for what, we do not know. So many of our ostensible "goals", so many of the things we think we want, turn out to be the masks behind which our real desires hide; they are the symbols for the actual values and qualities for which we hunger. They are not reducible to physical or material things, not even to a physical person; they are psychological qualities: love, truth, honesty, loyalty, purpose—something we can feel is noble, precious, and worthy of our devotion. We try to reduce all this to something physical—a house, a car, a better job, or a human being—but it doesn't work. Without realizing it, we are searching for the *Sacred*. And the sacred is not reducible to anything else. [p. 171]

For Johnson, love, truth, honesty, loyalty, and purpose exist as eternal "forms" or ideas irrespective of the human beings who embody them. But, in claiming that these things are not reducible to physical things, "not even to a physical person", Johnson is splitting the human person into two separate poles: the physical and the sacred. As a consequence, Eros is split into lust or agape. Lewis and, to some extent, Johnson see passionate love between two actual people as necessarily adulterous, and, therefore, duty is polarized against desire, sexual love is polarized against a self-giving love. Both writers are influenced by de Rougemont (1956) who applies a Freudian reading to myths: a myth, such as Tristan and Iseult, disguises unpalatable truths which we would rather not face. Just as, for Freud, the obscurity of a dream is a form of censorship, so, for de Rougemont, the myth disguises the fact that passion (seen as adulterous passion) is linked to death and "involves the destruction of anyone who yields themselves up to it". If passionate love is taken to be the same as an adulterous affair, it is seen as acting against Christian values. Eros is a pagan god, and, for de Rougemont and Lewis, the multiplicity of the pagan religions has been supplanted by the monotheism of Christianity. There is, for them, only one religious narrative.

Yet, in passionate love, we can experience sexual desire and the desire to serve the other in one and the same moment. Jung himself did not split psyche and soma in this way: while we can describe such things as mind and body, and recognize that these two are not the same, neither can they be split. Jung describes an intermediate area he termed "psychoid" for the transitional space in which psyche and soma meet.

Johnson, like Lewis, also falls into the dualism of need-love and gift-love. He says the West has much to learn from the East and, in the last sentence of the book (Johnson, 1983), claims that from the East,

> We can learn that the essence of love is not to use the other to make us happy but to serve and affirm the one we love. And we can discover, to our surprise, that what we have needed more than anything was not so much to be loved, as to love. [p. 201]

Surely, what we most deeply need and long to attain with the "Other", whether with the divine other as transcendent or immanent, or, indeed, with another person, is, above all, to be loved as we love and to love as we are loved.

So, in an attempt to reach beyond the polarization of duty and desire, of "need-love" and "gift-love", let us turn now to those tales that blur that distinction.

Layla and Majnun

In the mystical tradition of Sufism that flourished especially in Islam in the eighth century, we have a possibility of resolving this dualism. Here, we are given occasional glimpses of human, passionate love as being in itself a path to God. Nizami, a twelfth century Persian Sufi poet, retells an old Arabic legend of two lovers,

Qays and Layla, who meet when young and fall deeply in love with each other. Layla's family disapprove of the connection, the more so as Qays is now mad with love for Layla (Majnun means madman). Even when Majnun's father contrives to take him to Mecca so that his son can pray for divine release from the sufferings of love, Majnun prays otherwise:

> They tell me: abandon love, that is the path to recovery—but I can gain strength only through love. If love dies, so shall I . . . I ask thee, my God, I beseech thee, in all the godliness of thy divine nature and all the perfection of thy kingdom: let my love grow stronger, let it endure, even if I perish . . . If I am drunk with the wine of love, let me drink even more deeply. [Nizami, 1966, p. 27]

This strange prayer suggests that Majnun has lost all thought of self. Despite his plea the lovers are continually kept apart from each other. However, they remain faithful to each other and finally, after many sufferings, first Layla and then Majnun die of their longing. Only in death are the lovers able finally to escape the limitations of their ego. But it is a process that began in love: Nizami writes: "Love loosens the knots of being, love is liberation from the vortex of egotism" (*ibid.*, p. 176.) At the end of the tale, a friend sees in a dream the two lovers enjoying paradise together, united as one. Although the story at one level is a Romeo and Juliet type tale of human love, it describes that love as becoming stronger than death, transforming both lovers into something that partakes of the divine. They become immortal through their very love. At another level, of course, the tale is told as an allegory of the love of the soul for the Divine Beloved. Yet, by using a well-known story of two human lovers, and in words such as those above, Nizami honours human love. Human love, he seems to assert, can be seen not just as an allegory of divine love, not even just a practice for it: if it can transcend the limitations of purely narcissistic love it can render the lovers immortal. Their love participates in divine love itself.

The story is very hyperbolic, and elsewhere in it there is much dualism in relation to bodily and spiritual love, but the interesting thing is that Majnun, and, indeed, the poet himself through Majnun's voice, does not talk at all about the need for a lover to *give up* his love for his beloved in order to attain to lasting bliss: he has learnt to go beyond the limitations of his own ego, not from any spiritual teacher or teaching, but *from the love itself.*

Eros and Psyche

The Ancient Greek myth of Eros and Psyche is essentially a religious story, which, in Jungian terms, describes the journey of individuation. It is a Beauty and the Beast tale as told by Apuleius. A beautiful maiden, Psyche, is fated to wed a monster, who turns out to be none other than the god Eros. Psyche does not see her lover, this is not allowed her, and he comes to her only by night. One night, however, she breaks the taboo by lighting a lamp to see her lover, and in that very instant loses him. In order to win him back, she has to complete four impossible tasks set her by Eros's mother, Aphrodite. She achieves three, but at the very end fails, and it is Eros himself who breaks away from his mother in order to rescue her. Our story tells how the human psyche can become whole through a relationship with Love itself—divine Eros as the essence of relatedness—and how Love itself must in turn be humanized through its relationship to the human psyche in order for the archetype of relatedness to become whole. As such, it is very pertinent to our theme.

Neumann's interpretation describes the myth as a tale about the process of individuation, and I commend the work as such (Neumann, 1956). However, his reading of it is bedevilled by gendered language and assumptions. While he rightly sees it as a tale for both sexes, he describes it as being a story about the "feminine" psyche in men or women. Yet, we know that that men fall in love just as readily as women (a survey asking individuals about their experiences of falling in love found more men claiming to have had this experience than women!) and, when they do so, they do so directly *as men* and not indirectly from some "feminine" part of their psyche. I would, therefore, suggest that it is more useful to read the tale as detailing the particular form of individuation that is possible when the psyche (not a gendered part of the psyche) encounters Eros. We can then see the four labours not in terms of the work that the "feminine" psyche must undertake in order to transform its "masculine" energies, but, rather, as the specific tasks required of the psyche in all who find themselves called to that particular path of individuation. The exigencies of passionate love make new demands on us.

Psyche's first labour is to sort out a vast heap of beans and seeds before daybreak. This task, I suggest, in part represents the need to sort out what are appropriate and what inappropriate feelings in the experience of Eros. The story here suggests what is needed by someone in love when he or she experiences a great variety of different feelings all mixed up together. In such a situation, what is required is the faculty of discrimination, the task of sorting into categories the confused amalgam of experiences. As we have seen, all the various projections must be differentiated. For example, we might decide: this feeling belongs with my mother, that feeling fits the situation with my partner, and so on. I would see the help given to Psyche by the ants who work in the night not as a peculiarly *feminine* way of needing to think, as Neumann claims (we now have better evidence that women are just as adept at a conscious form of thinking as men), but, rather, that the conscious mind cannot sort out the entire pile but must let the unconscious, in the form of the natural instincts, work away at the problem. When falling in love produces problems that need to be dealt with in therapy, for example, the therapist is aware that the conscious process of sorting out feelings is only a tiny part of the work. The rest is done, whether outside or inside the sessions, by unconscious processes to be found in phenomena such as the transference and countertransference, dreams, fantasies, and sometimes in a new relationship to the arts— poetry, for example. Since passionate love has its roots in the instincts (whether companionate, sexual, or religious instincts), much of this process must be allowed to continue to operate mainly in the unconscious. Too much analysis could destroy the transformative potential of the event and cool off the intensity of "heat" produced by the feelings, especially at the beginning of a relationship. This alchemical "cooking" is an essential ingredient of love's transformation.

Psyche's second task is to fetch a wisp of wool from the golden fleece of a ferocious flock of sheep. These sheep "borrow fierce heat from the blazing sun and wild frenzy maddens them, so that . . . they vent their fury in the destruction of men" (Neumann, 1956, p. 43). Again, Neumann has this as symbolizing how the feminine psyche must deal with "destructive power of the masculine" that threatens it. I would rather see the nature of this task as making an allusion to the destructive power of love's frenzy. Burning jealousy, searing hatred, blazing fury constitute, as we have seen, the shadow side of passionate love. Psyche is warned that she can only achieve her task if she attempts it by night. In matters of Eros, the power problem must not be dealt with head on, and the primal force of one's own instincts cannot be subdued merely by force of will. The ego must await the stilling of the passions in order to win their treasure, and one can gain a little of their priceless energy if love's patience can bide its time and thus redeem their destructive powers.

The third task is to bring back a crystal jar filled with water from the stream that feeds the rivers of the Underworld. This stream flows from an immeasurably high peak guarded by fierce dragons. As Neumann describes, Psyche must contain a portion of the eternal stream of life, the fructifying waters of the unconscious, in her own tiny human life. When a person (man or woman) loves in this way, they are called to embody eternal love in their mortal, transient, all too human vessel. It is the story, eternally repeated, of the incarnation in which divine love is brought to earth and "made flesh". As the medieval carol sings of Mary:

> There is no rose of such vertu
> As is the rose that bare Jesu.
> For in this rose conteinèd was
> Heaven and earth in litel space.
> Res Miranda . . .

The impossible, "wondrous thing" that Psyche must achieve is to contain "heaven and earth in little space". In this impossible task she is helped by Zeus's eagle, who himself fetches the water on her behalf. A bird is one of the symbols of the Self: its flight symbolizes the flight of divine inspiration or intuition. The tale of Psyche and Eros tells us that love, being ultimately of divine origin (non-ego), cannot be seized by us: it is too lofty a thing. We can only be receptive to it as to a divine spark. Yet, if one can contain heaven and earth in little space in this way, then something eternal is won.

Psyche's last task is to bring back a casket containing a portion of the beauty of Persephone, Queen of the Underworld. She manages the heroic feat, but then, at the last moment, she is tempted to open the casket to take for herself some of the beauty that belongs to the Goddess of beauty. Psyche wishes to be beautiful in Eros's eyes to win his favour. But, as she opens the casket, a deathly sleep overcomes her: the result of this theft is total passivity. Yet, the myth seems to tell us that Psyche cannot but fail here. Neumann reads this as a delightfully feminine tendency intrinsic to the "feminine psyche" that provokes Eros into his rescue of her. But I think it is important to keep in mind that the fourth labour was a task, and that its nature, like the nature of the other three tasks, gives us an indication of the dangers that can beset this form of love. Thus, I suggest, the task can usefully be understood as the need to deal with the danger in love of merely desiring to be desired (see Young-Eisendrath, 1999). For women, there is indeed more temptation to identify with Beauty itself in order to win love, and, as Young-Eisendrath points out, the attempt to elicit desire in others can lead to a foreswearing of one's autonomy. In fact, I have found that the tale of Psyche appeals a lot to women because, as a story, it tells of a woman who actively seeks her lover and is not simply the passive recipient of desire. However, poor Psyche, having struggled against all the odds in the three impossible tasks, falls into this mistake.

The other mistake is in taking for herself divine, eternal qualities in order to be seen as worthy of being loved. No Greek tale could be blind to the danger of hubris in stealing what belongs to a god. We could say that this labour deals with the dangers of both positive (grandiose) and negative (self deprecating) inflation. Psyche thinks too little of herself: she desires only to be desired and, thus, falls prey to the dangers of archetypal identification. In an archetypal identification, the individual is lost. They become overwhelmed by the collective, just as Psyche is overwhelmed by the essence belonging to the goddess. Thus, Psyche becomes as one dead. She has lost autonomy and can no longer act for herself.

Yet, it would seem that no lover is entirely immune to this: idealization of the beloved can cause the lover to feel abject. Our story tells us that this fault in a man or woman can be redeemed by love itself. We mistakenly believe that we have to deserve love and try to win it by whatever means we can. But, if and when the desire to be desired is an (albeit mistaken) attempt to win love and the desire to be loved itself stems from mature love for the other, then love can beget love. Mutual respect and consideration can help to transform sado-masochistic dynamics. When we love another person maturely, we desire their wellbeing, and this must include some wish for them to have their autonomy. If Eros is at last to become Psyche's lover, he can no longer punish her for acting on her wish to see him as he really is. Her very failure stems from an act of love, and Love itself is forced to recognize it as such. We, too, must acknowledge a humility in love that can be deeply touching rather than masochistic. The lover puts themselves at the mercy of the beloved, and, if this is not defensive, this vulnerability provokes love in return. As Neumann relates, it is only at the point that Eros, wounded and mooching around in his mother's palace, realizes the strength of his love for Psyche that his love is able to override incestuous love. His wound seems to be now healed, and he goes off at last to find his bride and revive her. The corresponding danger in the beloved would be sadism: letting the lover "do all the running", basking in the warmth of the others idealizing projections, and not seeing the lover as a person in his or her own right. Then, the task of adapting to the other is left to the lover entirely, while the beloved simply remains where they are, enclosed in their own narcissistic world. But this is a love story, and Eros has been moved by Psyche's extraordinary efforts and comes to earth to meet her precisely *where she is*.

At the end of our tale, Zeus recognizes the power of Eros over him. He grants the god of love his desire: Psyche is brought to heaven. There, Zeus offers her the ambrosia of the gods saying, "Psyche, drink of this and be immortal." Psyche is promised that Eros shall never leave her arms, and her union with him shall endure forever.

To sum up, we learn from our tale that a love in which the lover succeeds in sorting out all the various projections and component parts of the confused mass of feelings; that can with patience endure the storm of destructive passions; that can prompt the lover to embody in their finite being a fragment of the divine, and that can love enough to risk death itself and the negative subjugation of self—such a love is worthy of that name. Such a love inspires love in return and thus manages to partake of the divine.

But, if human love partakes of something divine, if the lover might seem to incarnate divinity in some shape or form, and if, in loving, one is felt to be swept up into something beyond the merely human, how do we avoid a form of idolatry of the loved one? We have caught a glimpse of the divine and yet we are aware that our beloved is all too human. We will turn to the verse of the Persian poet, Rumi, who addresses this conundrum again and again in his work.

Rumi on love

Rumi's own story is extraordinary in itself. He was a highly respected Koranic scholar of his time, a religious teacher with his own disciples. However, when he met the man he later acknowledged as his teacher, a wondering dervish from Tabriz, he experienced the kind of love that went beyond anything he had previously known. When Shams disappeared for good, Rumi, disconsolate, was left to deal with this loss. The suffering of longing for, separation from, or loss of the beloved permeates much of his poetry, as do accounts of the joys and bliss of such a love. In time, the poet grows though this process to a point at which he eventually realizes, in practice and not merely intellectually, that he and his beloved are one. Rumi (1999) understands well the necessity for, and the value of, Love's incarnation. In quatrain 61, he insists,

> If you have illusions about heaven
> lose them.
> The soul heard of one attribute of Love
> and came to earth.
> A hundred attributes of heaven
> could not charm her back
> It is here the soul discovers
> the reality of Love. [p. 24]

Since incarnation involves an embodied existence, we must beware of sublimation. As a defence against our shadow, it is dangerous. Denied admission, desire will only return and this time by the back door. In quatrain 1300, Rumi (1984), warns,

> You say you have no sexual longing any more.
> You're one with the one you love.

This is dangerous.
Don't believe that I have a love like that.

If one day you see a picture of how you think,
you'll hate yourself, openly. [p. 19]

Rumi would seem to imply that at a certain point distinctions break down: in loving the human being, Rumi (1998) discovers that he also loves the divine; in loving the divine he loves others. This discovery can be extremely confusing to the mind. Rumi claims,

I am ashamed
To call this love human
And afraid of God
To call it divine. [p. 46]

To say his love is only human is to belittle it, but claiming it to be divine would make him an idolator. This confusion of the mind is, in fact, clarity at a deeper level. Indeed, love itself is without bounds or boundaries. Rumi (1984) expresses this in Quatrain 511, with words that sound almost like a sigh, an exhalation into bliss:

The clear bead at the centre changes everything.
There are no edges to my loving now [p. 10]

In other words, Rumi asserts the value of this life, even at the same time as he asserts the ultimate reality of the divine, as giving us the only chance we have to discover what love really is. The paradoxical nature of love cannot be fully understood by the discriminating mind (or Logos) and is best expressed in poetry or fable.

Last of all, with this in mind, we shall turn to a little story that expresses the paradox superbly. I will make no commentary on our tale, but let it speak for itself.

A Sufi parable

The Sufi scholar, Shah (1982), tells a story about a beautiful and wise young woman, Fahima, who once lived in the city of Basra. She was also wealthy, and she had many, many suitors. One day, a prince glimpsed her loveliness and wooed her most persistently. Being wise, she resisted his siege, although she did, in fact, like him.

Then, one day, she found herself captured and imprisoned by the prince, who was now trying to win her by force. She remained obdurate, and after many months he went on a journey to Baghdad, leaving Fahima behind in her prison. In Baghdad, he caught sight of a beautiful young woman who reminded him of Fahima. He wooed this lady and they were married. In time, the princess gave birth to a little girl, and the prince was delighted. After a while, however, he made another long journey, to Tripoli, leaving his new bride behind. And there again he saw a woman that he fell in love with. He wooed her and they were married. This princess had a little boy. Yet again, his wanderlust got the better of him and he journeyed to Alexandria, fell in love yet again, married this lady, and had a child by her. But, after a year or two, the prince felt home-sick for Basra and all he had left behind. He returned home to find Fahima still imprisoned. At this, his heart smote him, and he declared to Fahima that he still loved her and wanted to marry her, but had betrayed her terribly.

She asks him if he is prepared to tell her the whole truth. He agrees, but tells her it will make little difference: wise as she is, even *she* cannot find a way out of the mess he has made. Fahima responds by telling him that if he leaves nothing out of his story she may yet be able to find a solution. So he tells her the whole sorry tale and is full of regret. Thereupon, Fahima tells the prince to go to his rooms and await someone who would be announced shortly and whom he must admit. She withdraws, dresses in all her finery, and appears with the prince's three children. The prince is dumbfounded. Only then does he learn that Fahima was the same woman as each of the others he married, and that she is mother to all of his three chil-dren. She had found her own way to escape the prison earlier than he, and each time she had got wind of his intended journeys she contrived to arrive there before him and let him think he had discov-ered her afresh each time. The prince is delighted, reforms his character, and he and Fahima live happily ever after.

The inscape of the beloved other

I want to consider for a moment the conundrum that, in one sense, all our various love stories form one coherent whole and yet at the same time: we love a person best when we love them for who they uniquely are.

Shastri (2006), a Sanskrit scholar and teacher, uses the Sanskrit term "Tadatmata", that occurs often in the Vedas. Describing it, he writes,

> It means literally the substantial unity of the one with spiritual unity of the other. Take for instance many objects made of clay. There is a pot, there is a cow, a bird and a figure of a man, all made of clay. We can say there is Tadatmata between the figures of men and other objects made of clay and the clay itself . . .

> In Arabic literature, the classical example of lovers is that of Majnun and Leila. The Arab philosophers hold that love may begin with dwelling on individual characteristics but if it is true love, it will lead to Tadatmata between the two people concerned . . . Unless this Tadatmata exists between the lover and the beloved, the love is not permanent, not [nor] does it lead to the higher state of happiness and freedom . . . Science analyses objects, classifies them, discovers the unity which connects them all and calls it law, but by this method, which is purely empirical, science will never know the reality of an object which is only open to one who feels Tadatmata with it.

What is significant in this excerpt is again the idea that love between two people is not simply an *analogy* of the love of and for the divine, as in Lewis (1960), but that, if it touches the right levels, it can itself *participate in* the divine, may even lift the lovers into the sphere of the divine. As we have seen, Layla and Majnun, because of the very transcendence of their love, become immortal; they are lovers for all eternity. In legends, this is hinted at by motifs such as the two trees or rose bushes that spring from the graves of the lovers (who have died for their love), or that of the souls of both lovers rising from their graves together as birds, and so on. But note how the theme of immortality exists firmly in the context of a love that had become self-transcendent. In our tales, this is often demonstrated by the fact that either one or both of the lovers have been willing to give their lives for that love, or that they love beyond life itself. In psychological terms, this means that love must become a mature, a non-narcissistic version of love. In certain tales, this is symbolized by lovers' readiness to forfeit his or her possession of the beloved for a greater good. This is the case in *A Tale of Two Cities*, by Charles Dickens (1859), and in the film *Casablanca*. We note that the last two are examples of male sacrifice: what, then, is the female equivalent, since women are scarcely notably *less* self sacrificial than men? Person (1988) perspicaciously remarks (p. 119) that self sacrifice in love can take two different forms: the lover may renounce the beloved for the beloved's own good or for some other worthy cause, or he or she may stay in the relationship, sacrificing his or her own self-realization (and here we must translate this as ego fulfilment) for the sake of the relationship. She suggests that, to the extent that there is a gender difference, whatever the reason, men might be more likely to favour the former and women the latter.

And yet, when we love, we also know that what we love in the other would seem to be their essential uniqueness, that which is irreducible to anything else. This is how I understand the poet Hopkins's term "inscape", his own term for the "this-ness" of a thing: that which makes the individual what that individual uniquely is (see Catherine Philips' introduction, p. xx and p. xxiii in Hopkins [1986]). Somehow, we recognize in loving another that there is an essential oneness within which we find our connection, and yet at the same time when we love we love most of all what is unique to that person, what no one else could replace. Both are true. And, perhaps even stranger, both facts seem to be an essential truth discovered within the experience of falling in love. The divine is both one and many: most divine in that essential oneness; most divine in that essential diversity.

The benefits and dangers that derive from the religious narrative

In dealing with religious ideas or constructs, one is, to Jung's understanding, dealing with the given archetypes in the human psyche. When a person encounters archetypal material, whether in a dream or imagery or in outer life, there is often a sense of awe akin to a religious awe. Jung describes this quality as "numinous". As I have emphasized before, the archetypes are bigger than the ego: the gods are more powerful than we. The struggle to humanize the archetype is the eternal human problem, whether that is symbolized by a Greek myth such as the story of Psyche and Eros, or in a bible story such as Jacob's struggle with the angel. Sometimes, the struggle is a conflict; sometimes, it takes the form of a letting go. Either way, if we can face the conflict and see it through to its finish, we are transformed in the process. But it is precisely because archetypes are evoked that we are in danger of being overpowered by the experience.

If we return for a moment to the idea of basic core emotional operating systems correlating to certain association areas in the brain, we could hypothesize that there is likely to be an emotional operating system that at least roughly equates with the religious instinct. At a more intellectual level, the religious instinct might associate with a philosophical mode, with a tendency in human beings to try to discover the "why" of things, to wonder about our place in the universe, and so on. However, there is also a deeply emotional component to religious instinct that we might call "religious feeling". We have looked at the aesthetic mode, where religious feeling can be evoked by an experience of beauty, order, harmony, and so on: a beautiful sunset or choristers' song might produce feelings of longing, wonder, or awe. But there can also be a relational mode to religious experience, an I–Thou element to religious feelings, and I suggest that this experience is more akin to that of love. I consider it to be certainly very close to the experience of falling in love. It would seem to strike a particular note quite distinct from those struck by Fisher's three primary emotional systems in mating (1998, 2006). I wonder, therefore, if, in addition to these three, lust, attraction, and attachment, there might not be a fourth: an awed, at times even worshipful, form of love? It is the form of love that we give to something we see as transcending our personal selves, be it a person, a cause, or a group. Its transcendent, or felt transcendent, quality demands our commitment, our loyalty, even our service. There is felt to be a way in which our individual self is subsumed into that greater entity, a "You rather than me", a "Thy will be done". I would suggest that we could call this kind of love, *devotion*. It is a self-giving form of love and is often present in falling in love. But we must remember that even self-giving love has its monstrous side: the mother who "devours" her children in her complete giving over of herself to them; the terrorists who can kill others and even themselves in the name of religion; the national pride that cannot see beyond deadly versions of patriotism that lead to "ethnic cleansing", better termed genocide, and so on.

We saw how Newberg's experiments might suggest that de-afferation of the PSPL might lead to a sense of permeation or, at the extreme end of the spectrum, a dissolution of the ego's boundaries, and how falling in love might be a mid-point on a continuum of epistemic states of unitary being. One of the emotional factors common to both might be bliss: the bliss of subsuming the ego into something beyond it. The danger is that this bliss could become intoxicating, and even addictive. We have seen how many of the same neuro-chemicals and neural pathways are involved in both passionate love and addiction to psychotropic drugs, and some degree of addiction may explain the obsessional quality of falling in love.

So, while a religious narrative makes sense of why we so often find something sacred within human passionate love, the dangers, as highlighted by that same discourse, are to do with the shadow side of religion or, we could say, more generally of idealism (as opposed to idealization, which we looked at earlier). The faculty of reason has a rightful place among our other faculties and all our faculties are of value: all must act together for an individual to be able to make fully rounded ethical decisions. It is all too easy for intense passion to act unilaterally within the individual. Then, all moral debate is silenced and the most unspeakable crimes can be committed under the auspices of Love. This does not mean that Love itself is a false god, but that we need to be clear as to when it acts in accord with the totality of the human being or when it has cut itself off from other faculties, such as discrimination. In her book (2008), Pickering looks at "being in love" rather than "falling in love", as I do here. It is a helpful account of the painstaking work necessary in long-term committed relationships to guard against love being high-jacked by something else, something she identifies as narcissism. However, since, as we have seen, passion has a useful role, I would prefer to describe this particular danger as being a risk of the whole (person) being hi-jacked by the part.

Altogether, we have so far explored five main narratives that give meaning to the experience of falling in love and can do much to explain its tremendous power. Each of these narratives has something valuable to say and we do well to take all of these into account. But how do we put all these strands together? Are they compatible? Is love simply a "many-splintered" thing, as one reviewer of Jessica Benjamin's book put it, or is there some over-arching narrative that can bring all these disparate experiences and ways of describing them together?

PART II

LOVE'S ALCHEMY:
PUTTING IT ALL TOGETHER

CHAPTER SIX

Various dualisms and their synthesis

Do not confuse resignation with surrender,
There is a world of difference between the two:
When you resign yourself you leave
Your roaring, passionate self
Shut up inside your house;
Surrender is that passion

The multi-valency of passionate love

What we have seen from our exploration of the different narratives about passionate love is that many elements make up the phenomenon as a whole. Thus, it is a mistake to concentrate on only one or two narratives. Indeed, many of the dangers inherent in the experience may well stem from adopting too narrow an approach. This narrowness of approach can be destructive, whether it is in the lovers themselves, in the psychotherapist that either one (or both) of them might consult, or in the writings they may turn to. Winnicott reminded people that play, while first explored in depth psychology in relation to its role in therapeutic cure, is, none the less, a phenomenon in its own right and an important part of the life of the individual (and, we might add, of society). In a like manner, we need to remind ourselves that passionate love, while explored, as we have seen, in depth psychology first of all as "neurotic transference" and then as a therapeutic tool, is also a phenomenon in its own right and an important part of the life of the individual and of society. Falling in love, like making love, is very close to play.

We have sorted out, like Psyche with the seeds, some of the important components of passionate love as highlighted by the different accounts in our five chapters, but a full account of the phenomenon requires all of the narratives. There is a real danger in a "nothing but" attitude: for example, passionate love is nothing but sexual desire; or it is nothing but the need for a mate and/or the need for children; or that it is nothing but the recreation of loves in our childhoods; or nothing but an epiphenomenon of the brain and its chemical reactions; or that it is nothing but the need to integrate the Animus or Anima; or that, when viewed as romantic love, it is simply a means of subjugating women; that it is not anything to do with the particular person loved, but really desire for the divine; and so on. Each one of these accounts of passionate love is crucial to our understanding of the phenomenon as a whole; it can be, and perhaps most often is, all of these things, but if any one of these narratives is merely taken on its own, or allowed to become the definitive one, there is a danger of reduction. In so far as the experience is aptly described by any one narrative, it will present the particular dangers that we have already explored through the lens of each narrative, but perhaps the greatest single danger lies precisely in reductionism itself—to claim that love "is nothing but", or "really just", or "ultimately", or even "primarily" this or that. It is multi-layered and, further, it will be different things in different contexts. Which, if any, aspect is given more prominence will vary from society to society, from age to age, and from person to person, as well as at different times in the life-span of any one individual.

A question of personality type will also come into this, for example, a sensation type might well see falling in love as something purely pragmatic, an attraction that serves one in finding a mate or companion, for example. An intuitive type might see it as something essentially symbolic of something else that is going on, feeling types might attach too much importance to it as a feeling, thinking types too little. The extrovert may see it only as a means to relate to another, the introvert as only a means to grow as an individual. It is also of value to remember Jung's suggestion that our shadow function (feeling for the thinking type and, vice versa, sensation for the intuitive type and, vice versa, extroversion for the introverted type, and vice versa) is often the very function through which we are called into individuation. For a full elaboration as to how one's typology in this regard influences one's theories, see Jung (1971) and von Franz and Hillman (1971).

The balance and tension between the various polarities

A second mistake is to reduce falling in love to just one pole of a pair of opposites. There are a range of possible pairs of opposites which are constellated in falling in love; indeed, this seems to be one of the most striking symptoms, and various different narratives might risk overemphasizing one or the other pole. Some of these narratives we have already examined: there is the inner–outer polarity, with the emphasis on the intrapsychic aspect of the person (psychoanalysis) or on the interpsychic (relational psychologies); the nature–nurture polarity, with the emphasis on the given-ness of human nature (the sciences) or on the influence of the environment (depth psychology generally); there is the retrospective–prospective polarity, with the emphasis on where we come from (developmental narratives) or where we are going (teleological narratives). Also implicit in these narratives is an emphasis on the one pole of other pairs of opposites, such as mind and body, body and soul, secular and religious, natural and supernatural. I hope that I have been able to show that, by exploring the main narratives, we can see that each of these has something important to say. We can go further, and will be in a better position to avoid the danger of losing the balance and tension between the various opposites, if we take full account of all of these narratives as a whole.

But there remain other accounts that risk reducing falling in love to one or other pole of various pairs of opposites, some of which we have only just touched on. Among these pairs of opposites are: the individual and society, self-abnegation and surrender, need-love and gift love, human love and divine love, and, finally, bondage and liberation. I will explore these accounts in the remainder of the chapter.

The individual and society

Carotenuto (1989) describes how love, having profoundly transformative potential, confronts society as something dangerous. Desire has the potential to take us away from the beaten track into entirely new territory. This fact can inspire fear. He writes,

> Whenever one rejects the experience of love by rationalizing it away, one is obeying a collective law that has been internalized. We have all absorbed this law that negates the free realization of desire in the face of life's continuous invitations. Thus, while life conspires to arouse us, it can—and does—often happen that we deny our desire in obedience to an external veto that by now is fatally alive within us without our even being conscious of it. [p. 29]

This veto he terms the "voice of conscience", whose function is to "prevent the anguish and forestall the terrible feeling of being hunted" when we do something others could disapprove of (*ibid.*, p. 30). Thus, to keep from feeling guilty, we respect the veto which in turn keeps the violence of desire at a distance. The conflict he describes is really none other than the old chestnut: that of duty *vs.* desire. And, while Carotenuto is inspiring on the value of love–desire, and has much to say that is helpful on the subject, I do not think conscience is quite so simple an affair and quite so easily dismissed. If that were so, why would *Casablanca*, as we have seen, be one of the best loved of all romantic films, a story that has the hero forgoing the fulfilment of his own love–desire for something more noble?

In a situation of moral conflict, I think we can bring more light to bear on this subject if we use Jung's (1958) distinction between conscience as the internalized collective moral code, that is, the superego as defined by Freud, and conscience as an inner voice. A developed conscience, then, is more than a set of rules. It is something elaborated, worked out and worked upon, a highly differentiated thing born out of the wisdom derived from lived experience, and is the fruit of long exposure to multiple and specific instances of morality. (See Hughes [2004].) Jung terms the former "moral", in that it is based on *mores*, and the latter "ethical", in that it is based on one's *ethos*. The ethical aspect of conscience is reflective and comes into play

> when two decisions or ways of acting, both affirmed to be moral and therefore regarded as "duties", collide with one another. In these cases, not foreseen by the moral code because they are mostly very individual, a judgement is required which cannot properly be called "moral" or in accord with custom. [Jung, 1958, par. 856]

It is the conflict between two good options that necessitates our conscious scrutiny of the problem and, therefore, calls for a degree of individuation. A person with an individuated conscience does not turn to the superego as the highest court of appeal, but must test the dictates of the superego against this inner voice. My sense is that Freud was closer to this sense of conscience with his term "ego ideal", but he often conflates the two. Perhaps Jung could be charged with giving too little weight to *vox populi* in practice, but his distinction remains sound. I would want to emphasize that an ethical judgement in such a conflict of two goods must give full and due consideration both to the collective and to the individual voice. If either of these is silenced, then one is in danger of making either too collective or too individualized (rather than individual) a decision.

Falling in love can throw us headlong into this most profound of all conflicts. If, as Jung suggests, in any important conflict we are able to hold ourselves in the tension between the opposites, give each its value, and try to grow beyond to some third thing that is born out of the conflict of the opposites, then there will be true transformation. The film, *The Bridges of Madison County*, mentioned previously (Chapter Four), manages to honour both the extraordinarily transformative nature of the love between the married woman and the artist *and* her own genuine values of commitment to her husband and her marriage and children. Although, as in *Casablanca*, there is the same theme of sacrifice, in *The Bridges of Madison County* the mutual transformation of the two lovers is explored in much greater depth. The particularity of conscience is very beautifully evidenced by the fact that Francesca's love story, read by her children only after her death, inspires a very different life choice in each. Both of the adult children are struggling in their marriages, but the son is inspired by his mother's story to return to his marriage to try harder, and the daughter to leave hers. In other words, what is right must depend upon the detail and context of the individual situation.

In those modalities of psychotherapy that pay attention to transference and countertransference dynamics and work with them, it is clearly demonstrated how permission for Eros to have its place within the therapist–patient relationship, together with the maintenance of the erotic boundaries between them, actually enhances the growth of the patient and, in all likelihood, that of the therapist/analyst also. Conversely, both within and outside of the therapeutic relationship, *denial* of sexual attraction, where it exists, or a *reactive enactment* of it, are actually *two different ways of achieving the same end: a flight from the tension of opposites*. In this case, the particular tension is likely to be between acting and not acting on sexual desire. In a workshop for training therapists, one participant told me, "I couldn't ever fall in love with a client as that would be too dangerous." Until that moment, he had been unable to see that there could be a choice not to act out of sexual desire. Or it might be for someone that they actually do not, in practice, experience any choice. Hence, desire could only be suppressed. His assumption had been completely unconscious until it was flushed out by the discussion of sexual feelings in the consulting room. As depth psychology teaches us, we are far more susceptible to being taken over by impulses that are unconscious than by those that have been made conscious. This awareness is not just cerebral: it must stem from experience also. Only by developing the capacity to allow feelings to have their own life (to some extent, thereby, unlearning the inhibitions of childhood) and by developing the capacity to constrain them when needed (learning authentic inhibitions) can we find the proper synthesis of duty and desire.

And passionate love particularly, especially if illicit in any way, poses this paradox: that the very love that impels the lovers towards transgression of the boundaries also teaches them the transformative truth that no human being is an island, but exists as part of a whole. This conflict demands a degree of individuation. Only by a highly nuanced, adequately felt, and thoroughly reflected upon readiness to live within the conflict and to take into account, as far as one can, all the desires of all those involved, including one's own, can a genuine and authentic morality be maintained. Such a stance will attempt to honour both the value of the love between the two people and the wisdom that this love can bring in discovering one's interconnectedness with others. As Jung has shown with his idea of the transcendent function, we can cheat our way round a serious conflict by taking a short-cut and denying proper weight to one or other aspect of the polarity. Thus, a simple rule, "duty over desire", would be used to avoid the tension of the opposites that would be uncovered by giving due attention to the desire, just as a simple reaction; "desire over duty" avoids the tension of the opposites that duty brings to bear. Only the life lived authentically in the tension between the opposites produces growth beyond the duality.

Self-abnegation and surrender

Person (1988) makes the important distinction between surrender and submission. In the former, the impulse is from within; its purpose is "self-purification or self-expansion through the transcending of the self and identification with the attributes of the Other" (p. 146). No self-will stands in the way: it is unforced and it has no covert agenda, such as manipulation. By contrast, in submission one is attempting to control a superior and dominating force, and to preserve one's will and autonomy in so far as one can. Submission implies an external dominant force, real or imagined; it also has a covert agenda to manipulate the "Other" in order to maintain the self.

Person gives some very instructive instances of when surrender is less to do with the wish for self-transcendence and more to do with "conscious or unconscious feelings of inadequacy, dependency, powerlessness, even worthlessness, and the need to counter them". The aims of such a surrender are, then,

> the bolstering of a fragile self, the restoration of a damaged self, the glorification of an impoverished self, the cohesion of a fragmented self, the empowering of a powerless self, or the obliteration of a hated self. When love is motivated by aims such as these it is

regressive rather than progressive—an attempt to secure the protection and support longed for early in life. [*ibid.*, p. 147]

But here we have some dualism in this polarization of past *vs.* future, that is, regressive *vs.* progressive. For Jung, there was such a thing as the backward step for leaping forward ("reculer pour mieux sauter"). Regression might be the only way to progress, and we might be called into growth or "self-transcendence" by our very pathologies. Rather than the term "self-transcendence", which, to me, has the connotation of leaving something of one's self behind, I prefer the idea of *wholeness*: in Person's term "self-transcendence" for *self*, one must substitute *ego*. As we have seen, the ego, whether as function or as complex, is only a part of the whole self where that is seen as the totality of conscious and unconscious, personal and collective. Therefore, when the ego, acting alone, directs the destiny of the total individual, that destiny becomes too narrow. Consciousness must be informed by the unconscious and relate to it as an equal and opposite "Other". Thus, the ego is in dialogue with this Other, and this relationship of ego and unconscious comprises the total self.

Furthermore, the ego must first be developed properly before it can begin to act as an effective executive for the whole self. The self-transcendence Person refers to presupposes a degree of ego development, otherwise we have a case of defensive sublimation. Just as a pear will fall from the tree when ripe and produce (in nature, if not in horticulture) new fruit trees, so the ego, if development progresses naturally, matures, ripens, and fulfils its task of bringing something larger than itself to birth. As King Lear says in Shakespeare's play, "ripeness is all". To desire "self-transcendence" without allowing for the fact that the ego needs to be mature is like stripping the pear from the tree in order to plant its unripe seeds, which, as we know, would then have no chance at all of developing. To claim that the birth of a new plant first requires the full development of the seed of the parent plant does not represent any dualism between seedling and seed. It is just a question of a different emphasis, depending on the particular stage involved.

Thus, if we make the distinction between *ego-fulfilment*, as fulfilment of only a *part* of the personality as a whole, and *self-fulfilment*, as the fulfilment of the *whole* self (Self), then "self-fulfilment" would be a better term here than self-transcendence.

Need-love and gift-love

Closely connected to the above polarity is one that Lewis (1960) posits as 'need-love' *vs.* 'gift-love'. His exploration of the two is subtly nuanced: even gift-love such as the gift-love of a parent for his or her children or of a professor for her or his student can turn voracious: you *must* receive from me what I have to give you (pp. 48–49). Such love does not allow the protégé to grow up and grow away from them. For Lewis, it is a "higher love", a love that desires the good of the object as such, from whatever sources that good comes and not only from oneself, that must step in and help or tame the instinct before it can let go in this way. Here, again, is the assumption that this "higher love" is not instinctual. Yet, we know that instinct is also involved when a mother bird pushes her chick out of the nest. The human mother who proudly but tearfully sees her child off at the school gates on their first day at school is not torn between an instinctive love and a spiritual love when she sincerely wishes them a contemporary version of "God speed" at the same time that she yearns to keep them back. She is torn between two different aspects of the *same* instinct: it is a form of the mothering instinct in both cases, but one aspect of that instinct is better suited to a younger child and the other to an older one. The action needs to be in keeping with the child's stage of development. Thus, rather than higher and lower loves, I think the more useful distinction is between age-, or rather, stage-appropriate love and love that is inappropriate for any one stage of development. More generally, the most effective love would be that which is in tune with the person and their genuine needs. This idea takes us closer to Bowlby's "attuned response". A mother's difficulty when she holds on to her children excessively is not exactly that she does not let them go, but, rather, that she does not let them grow. After all, she will never cease to be a mother to these children, even in their maturity. Senility might, at the end, reverse the roles, but not the fact of that relationship. Rather than "higher" *vs.* "lower" love, or self-regarding *vs.* other-regarding love, we have attuned love (attuned both to self *and* others) *vs.* non-attuned love.

Having made this somewhat hierarchical distinction, Lewis later acknowledges that Eros obliterates the distinction between need-love and gift-love (p. 91.) While he sees this fact, he misses its significance. What he must, perforce, admit is that Eros can give us a glimpse of a situation in which our good and that of the other have become one and the same thing. This, I believe, is not simply a peculiar condition of Eros that only pertains as long as passionate love endures. It reveals a strange truth: it is at least *possible* to experience giving to another as a need as passionate as any other passionate desire. More: it is at least possible to come to a point where giving and receiving become indistinguishable; that there may yet be a place where the dog-eat-dog world of conflicting self interests does not obtain. Passionate love may help us to reach this point. It does not *necessarily* help us to remain there, and yet it may. We *might* find the experienced possibility of delight in putting one particular person's good on a par with (or even above) our own gives us an imagined possibility that this could be the case with others.

This odd paradox is described by John Stuart Mill in his *Autobiography* (1873). After what he cites as a "crisis" in his "mental history", a period of serious depression, Mill asks himself what is happiness and concludes:

> Those only are happy (I thought) who have their minds fixed on some object other than their own happiness; on the happiness of others, on the improvement of mankind, even on some art or pursuit, followed not as a means, but as itself an ideal end. Aiming thus at something else, they find happiness by the way.

Of course, Mill's view could be criticized as relating only to externals. If, however, we again make the important distinction between ego-fulfilment and self-fulfilment, it makes sense that it is the absorption of the ego in something other, *whether internal or external to it*, that can, as a by-product, give happiness or wellbeing or self-fulfilment. The external Other may indeed be a cause, a work of art, love of another human being, and so on, but the internal Other might be the objective Self or aspects of the impersonal unconscious such as the Inner Partner. I think that it is the quality of self-absorption (more technically, ego-absorption)—the ability to be utterly lost in something—that provides the self-fulfilment here. Thus, to paraphrase Jesus' words, the ego finds its greatest fulfilment in losing itself. Passionate love can have much to teach us about such a losing of self (ego) and finding of self (Self).

Human and divine love

Some versions of religious narrative can fall into the error of employing dualistic language when describing the love of one human being for another: they stress that when a person falls in love, it is not the object of one's love that one loves; it is the divine. At worst, one is enjoined to learn detachment from the particular love of this particular person. At best, this human love is seen as a practice for the other, divine love. It is as if they would say, "you must love God (that is, God transcendent, God "in the sky", so to speak) *rather than* the human being who is 'only' an image of the divine". Yet, to any passionate lover, this is a travesty of what their love would tell them. Often, in the act of falling in love, there is a sense, conscious or unconscious, of loving something divine. Where idealization is not pathological, then this quality is seen as some form of divinity within the other; sometimes that divinity irradiates the beloved for the lover. The lover cannot or will not say, "I love the soul of this person, but not their body", and any love worth its name cannot say the reverse either: "I love the body of this person but not their soul". The psychoanalytic version of dualistic thinking is to say that the lover is simply transferring love due to parents on to the love object; the equivalent in analytical psychology might be to say the person is simply projecting their Animus or Anima on to the loved one. But this would be to suggest that, in passionate love, the beloved is never seen for what they are. Clearly, those projections that we have put on to the beloved that do not in any way belong to him or her are distortions; they prevent us from seeing the other clearly, and, over time, need to be withdrawn and taken back in as parts of the self. But there are two things that should be borne in mind: first, that it is the beloved who has, in a sense, allowed us to discover those aspects of ourselves through projection and who has, thus, helped to give us back to ourselves (as long as the projections have not been too destructive in the process), and second, we need to ask ourselves what is it that passionate love allows us to see that should *not* be taken back? What is it that we cannot possess?

I would suggest that it is not so much the *loved one* who does not belong to the lover: there is, after all, again a paradox in love that, while the beloved can never be taken possession of, yet, in reciprocal love, each lover is giving something of themselves to the other. Rather, it is the *love itself* that the lovers cannot appropriate: it is the love itself that is "of the divine": love is an archetype and relates to instinct, whether that is seen as a social, a spiritual, or a sexual instinct. In all of our earlier explorations, through the different narratives of passionate love, one way or another, we have seen again and again how Eros is, as lovers might put it, "bigger than the two of us". Whether that supraordinate fact be the mating instinct and the concomitant powerful brain chemistry, powerful dynamics in the psyche from the earliest months of life, or the deepest of spiritual longings for union and a release from alienation, or even just the reality of the beloved her- or himself, it remains bigger than any one person's ego. The love that has been brought into being by the chemistry (or alchemy) between the two lovers is bigger than either lover or beloved. This is analogous to the way in which a child born of the physical expression of passionate love is more than either one of the lovers. Lewis (1960) warned against treating Eros as a god. But I think it is not Love itself that must be dethroned, but the little ego who wishes to arrogate to itself the power of the gods. Hubris, not Eros, is the moral problem here.

As with the painter–poet Gibran, who says of his muse, "If only I could paint her as beautiful as she really is", so the lover has an intuition that, in their love for the beloved, they are being given a glimpse of how their beloved truly is. This conviction will, of course, most often fade with the fading of passion, and, for this reason, the cynic will simply see the lover as having been deluded. But this might not be the whole truth. In intensely passionate love, the statement, "I love him" or "I love her" may be deluded and, therefore, dangerous, but perhaps not so much because it is not really the beloved themselves that the lover loves (although, of course, when there is a great deal of projection that will be the case) as because it is not, in the end, "I" who loves. Perhaps proper clear-sighted love, which sees the beloved as they truly are, is indeed love, because it does not come only from the ego of the person but from something approaching the total self, and because it loves not only the ego of the beloved but also the beloved's totality. The danger, again, is in a "nothing but" mentality: in passionate love, the "I" of the lover loves the "I" of the beloved, but the lover's unconscious is also involved, as is the beloved's unconscious. Thus, the love also may be a love of Self for Self. Perhaps we call it "falling in love" because we intuit a sense in which the ego "falls" into an experience of the Self. This very coming together of ego and Self is itself transformative.

Intimate and passionate love between two people could be seen as parallel to specializing in a given subject. If a student of history were to set out, for example, to cover the whole of world history, they could only hope to acquire a superficial understanding of their subject, but if they study a particular period in a particular area in depth, then the in-depth study will also teach them a great deal about the methodology and the nature of history itself as a whole. In specializing in depth, so to speak, through the love of and for one particular person, one can also glimpse love for the whole. To quote Rumi (1995),

> This moment this love comes to rest in me,
> many beings in one being.
> In one wheat-grain a thousand sheaf stacks.
> Inside the needle's eye, a turning night of stars. [p. 278]

A whole universe contained in *this* love, in *this* moment. Again: heaven and earth in little space. The macrocosm is reflected in the microcosm and, indeed, vice versa, or, as it has been put succinctly, as above, so below.

Bondage and liberation

And so we come to the last set of polarities that I want to examine, and the one that informs the title of this work. The practice of psychotherapy has as one of its implicit or explicit goals an enhancement of the degrees of freedom available to a person. We see ill-health as a narrowing of possibility by complexes that decrease our range of options of thinking, imagining, acting, and feeling. Yet, we also have to acknowledge, as many studies are increasingly showing, that happiness does not seem to increase with an increase in the ability simply to do what one wants. Does this not involve something of a contradiction?

Part of the solution to this problem lies again in a differentiation between the part and the whole. We may have the psychological situation where a person (at the ego level) is under severe constraint. Choices may not be available to them because a complex, acting as if a miniature personality within, has taken over the direction of the psyche as a whole. Again, development of the ego requires a degree of freedom from coercion by complexes. But, as we have seen, the freedom from self to be found in self- (i.e., ego-) transcendence can bring joy. Correspondingly, the restraints on the ego imposed by the dictates of the Self, whether those be the pricks of authentic conscience or the dictates of one's ordinary human needs (often now termed human givens), or constraints imposed by archetypes, can also bring joy. It is a question of who, or what, is doing the restraining!

Benjamin (1988), in the title of her book, *The Bonds of Love*, plays on the two connotations—positive and negative—of the word "bond". She demonstrates how relationship bonds have a value that is now too much underplayed in our Western society and has, as we have seen, also been underplayed in the psychoanalytic discourse. Freedom takes its value not only in the context of freedom *from* something negatively constraining, but also in the freedom *for* commitment to a person, a cause, a value, a piece of work, and so on. Even in an experience that I might find humiliating, for example, if I find that I am not loved where I love, if I, none the less, assent to the reality of that particular experience, the experience *I am actually having*, then it can still be transformative and, while constraining me severely, may also provoke a liberation.

So, we take up the question posed in the title of this book: is falling in love an experience of bondage or liberation? The answer must be both. Falling in love may, as I hope to have shown, be a means, one path among others, of individuation, and individuation is a synthesis of constraint and freedom. There is the issue of constraint and freedom in the inner world and constraint and freedom in the external world. Internally, we have the constraint of the ego to the Self as a supraordinate reality, and the freedom in the possibility of becoming most fully who we are. Externally, we have the constraint of a self acting in a world of other selves when needs collide and the freedom discovered with delight when our needs and the needs of other coincide. In outer relationships, there can be both a negative bondage, as in masochistic or obsessive relationship to the beloved, where the lover is too dependent on the beloved, and a negative liberation, as in defensive, avoidantly-attached styles of relating, where the lover is too independent of the beloved. There also can be a positive, healthy bonding where ties of affection are woven out of passion and a healthy freedom, where each partner is allowed the freedom to develop in the way they most need. Similarly, Bowlby demonstrated that the more that attachments needs are met in babyhood, the better (that is, deeper, more satisfying and more extensive) will be the relationships in later life. The "bonds of love" can tie us positively to those we love; they can root us with a particular person, in a particular time, and particular place, and that very limitation can contain within it the seeds of liberation..

Conclusion

Overall, we must be very aware of the dangers in the tendency to prefer one particular form of narrative over another and of preferring one pole of the pair of opposites over the other. We have seen from Jung how opposites must be resolved by holding the tension between them until the "third thing" that reconciles them is allowed to emerge. Often a polarity is contained in the opposing narratives. As we have seen, the developmental psychology *vs.* transpersonal psychology debate reflects the polarization between a causal or a teleological bias (past or future); the nature/nurture debate reflects the polarization between a bias towards internal or external influences; the psychoanalysis *vs.* the relational psychologies debate reflects a version of a polarization between individual and society; and versions that tend towards polarization of "selfless" and "selfish" love reflect the debate between religious idealism and psychoanalytic denigration.

I would want to argue, above all, that one of the best ways in which we can guard against the extremes of error in any one approach is by allowing for love's multiplicity: passionate love is indeed "a many-splendoured" thing. Multi-faceted, polymorphous, fragmented, many-layered, or whatever else, its glory lies in that it cannot be reduced to any one component. No one narrative is enough.

CHAPTER SEVEN

Holistic love: what difference does all of this make?

"This moment this love comes to rest in me,
many beings in one being.
In one wheat-grain a thousand sheaf stacks.
Inside the needle's eye, a turning night of stars"

(Rumi, 1995)

B efore we take up the theme of what difference a holistic picture of passionate love makes, I would first like to revisit two themes in the light of this new picture.

Transitional space revisited

This, then, is the place to return to Winnicott's idea of transitional space and see its relevance in the world of adult love. Winnicott describes how, for the baby, the first "not-me" possession occupies a space that is between the outer world of objects and the inner, psychic world; between the self and the not-self; between self and other. I would like to suggest that in falling in love we can be transported once again, *but this time in full maturity*, to this realm. Lovers know that they inhabit this transitional space, that it belongs to them, and that they also create it from their own love-filled imaginings. In one of the most well-known love songs, one that has endured for over half a century, "Somewhere" from the musical *West Side Story* (Sondheim, 1956), a girl sings of a place where lovers can be at peace together.

Of course, one of the reasons why the words are so poignant is because *West Side Story*, based as it is on Shakespeare's *Romeo and Juliet*, tells how, for the two central characters, there is no place for them to be together in a world full of the conflicts which separate them. Does this then mean that the place they long to be able to inhabit together, and dream is possible, does not exist? And yet, if we are honest, we recognize in ourselves something of what this longing is. It is the place symbolized by the point of intersection of the two worlds, as we explored in Chapter Four, for Pullman's lovers (1995). It is the place where the familiar Oxford-that-is, where Will lives, momentarily overlaps with the Oxford-that-might-have-been, where Lyra lives. It is that point of intersection symbolized by the bench in the Botanical Gardens where each, in his or her own world, has pledged to sit at the same time of the year and feel the presence of the other, although entirely separated by being in different worlds. It is the point of intersection between the night world of Isabeau and the day world of Navarre in *Ladyhawke*, when they can finally meet at last at the time of the solar eclipse. It is the twilight where the day boy and the night girl can both survive in MacDonald's (1961) fairy tale.

Rumi (1984), too, describes it hauntingly in one of his poems, quatrain 158:

> Out beyond ideas of wrongdoing and rightdoing,
> there is a field. I'll meet you there.
>
> When the soul lies down in that grass,
> the world is too full to talk about.
> Ideas, language, even the phrase *each other*
> doesn't make any sense. [p. 8]

This world exists neither wholly without nor wholly within; it exists within the *mundus imaginalis* that Jung describes, borrowing the phrase from Henry Corbin. This imaginal realm is the third thing between body and spirit: the world of the imagination, a world in which images are real, imaginal not "imaginary", which is now a word we use to mean the opposite of real. Jung describes this transitional space as the *temenos*, the sacred space between the inner psychological reality and outer material reality. Mythically, it is paradise, but a paradise regained *after* the awakening of self consciousness and of knowledge of sex and the polarities of good and evil. It is the place where heaven and earth meet, where Adam and Eve can wander freely with the animals once again, where they can converse with God. It is perhaps where there is even a regained innocence in their mature sexuality because it serves love.

Of course, in the lovers' desire to find this place, a place that is often described as being just for them, there may be a quality of wish-fulfilment, the yearning to escape from the vicissitudes of everyday life and conflict. But in this case it is a desire to go *back* to paradise rather than to engage in the tremendous and redemptive task of regaining it. It is noticeable that lovers, again and again, especially, but not only, when there are obstacles to their being together in the everyday outer world, dream of this special place where they can be together with no restrictions. Kalsched (1996) writes so evocatively and accurately about how the dissociative type of personality will create a provisional world like the Beast's palace when Beauty first arrives, where every need is met in a world of fantasy. This is not the imaginal world, the realm of imagination; it is a world of self-soothing fantasy. To create in the imaginal world takes effort: it is to construct a form of reality, albeit an "inner reality". Note how, near the beginning of the fairy tale, Beauty inhabits this fantasy world where her every wish is granted her before she even desires it. Yet, she has no real knowledge of her lover: she does not know what kind of being he is; she has not even set eyes on him. This is not clear-sighted love based on knowledge, but blind love based on fantasy. If the imaginal is the opposite of the imaginary, as Corbin thought, then the desire to escape life rather than to engage with it is what may draw a person into the world of illusion. This is illusion as "delusion", rather than illusion as natural play. (See Winnicott [1971].)

An important difference between the imagination and fantasy is that, in the first, the ego takes no control over those images. They are allowed their own spontaneous life in the psyche. In all but exceptional cases, we do not control our dreams, although, as we become more and more conscious of how the dream world works and of its laws (and there are, indeed, laws within this world), we can become more aware of how to make choices as the dream "I" within this world. In our dreams and in active imagination, we can increasingly transform the inner landscape, the dream narrative, as the dream ego increasingly begins to make different choices. But the non-ego characters, the unconscious components of the psyche, must be allowed their own autonomy, just as the dream world itself must be allowed its autonomy. Hence, we cannot know what effect the actions of the dream ego will have on the other dream characters. Indeed, the wonderful thing about the dream or imaginal world is that it is full of surprises. Fantasy, by contrast, never takes us by surprise.

Having said this, any therapist will recognize a particular form of lucid dreaming where there is a kind of control exercised by the vestiges of the ego, the dream "I", over the other dream figures. One notes this in the countertransference: there is a kind of "too good to be true" feel to the dream outcome, a sense of artificiality, of its perhaps having been forced. The patient telling one the dream also may feel somehow that it lacks conviction. By contrast, dreams that have managed to turn around deep-seated complexes have a quality of surprise to them: there is, especially to the dreamer, a wondrous feeling of breakthrough, a certain freshness, a vitality to them that cannot be faked. The therapist senses these qualities in the countertransference. The therapist, too, needs to be free of the bias of a wish-fulfilling desire that might try to interpret the dream on the basis of the "cure" they would like for their patient. But, equally, they might need to be alert to the tendency to fear, and hence deny, or to be too cynical of, and hence to disparage, transformations that might be judged to be "too good to be true". Again, it is the therapist's countertransference and their experience of the feeling quality of the dream that can guide him or her in this.

It would seem that, at times, passionate love itself can also have the power to create realities in the imaginal world. These realities, in having been given some form of inner life, have the power to change the outer world. When the Montagues and the Capulets, the warring families of Romeo and Juliet, bury the hatchet at the end of the tragedy, paradoxically the lovers, now dead, have in fact managed to create, through their passion for each other, the very *reality* in which there actually could now be a(n outer) "place" for them. This does not happen only in literature: there have been examples of this real life. The tragedy, of course, it is that it is too late for the two lovers: they are now both dead. But what Shakespeare's play also demonstrates is the truth that "love is stronger than death". Love has been able to redeem something in the outer world as well as in the inner.

Pullman would seem to intuit this in his own version of the Adam and Eve myth (Pullman, 1995). As we saw in Chapter Four, he introduces a kind of reversal of the myth. He makes the very moment of consummation of love between his Lyra and Will (whatever form that consummation takes) the point at which the world is redeemed. All vitality has been sapped from the world by dissociation (symbolized by the knife that is capable of severing whole worlds), but the outward flow is reversed once the lovers come together. Pullman imagines the possibility that passionate love introduces not death, pain, and sin, as in the myth of the fall, or at least not those things alone, but life, joy, and renewal. This is the knowledge of lovers of which even the gods are jealous. At the very least, there is actually nothing that the gods can really give to mortals who can love like this. In Ovid's *Metamorphoses*, Jupiter visits the world of humans in disguise to see if the sacred art of hospitality is still alive. Only an old couple, Philemon and Baucis, receive him as a guest should be received. In reward, he promises to grant them whatever wish they have. But their love for each other is such that for them the greatest gift he can give is simply that they be allowed to die together. Each, thinking of the other, does not want that other to feel the pain of separation. Furthermore, in the very nature of their request, both Philemon and Baucis acknowledge also the reality of death. They do not seek to escape it. There is no wish-fulfilling fantasy here. Death itself, far from dividing the couple, creates a transitional space. Winnicott (1971), describes play as a transitional phenomenon and claims:

> on the basis of playing is built the whole of man's experiential existence. No longer are we either introvert or extrovert. We experience life in the area of transitional phenomena, in the exciting interweave of subjectivity and objective observation, and in an area that

is intermediate between the inner reality of the individual and the shared reality of the world that is external to individuals. [p. 64]

Where can we go from here?
Practical considerations for psychotherapy

We have looked at how falling in love is a multi-faceted experience that needs a "portfolio" of discourses to do it full justice, and that no one narrative alone will suffice. We have looked at the pitfalls inherent in each aspect of passionate love and also at the dangers of emphasizing only one of those aspects, or, at least, of giving too much emphasis to any one aspect and not sufficiently taking the others into account. We have seen how the experience constellates many pairs of opposites and, at the same time, can provide the means to synthesize them. We have seen how only when all of the aspects of the experience are taken into account can we do justice to it as a whole. But the most important synthesis of all, I would suggest, is that of ourselves. It is not that we have to guard against the intensity or impulsivity of the feelings in falling in love, nor its obsessive quality, nor the experience of narcissism, nor love's addictive quality. Rather, I suggest, we do best to allow all of these experiences, the feelings, the fantasies, and the splinter personalities within, as parts of ourselves. As I have maintained earlier, the dangers of the phenomenon relate not to the emergence of all these shadow elements, but to the denial of them. Whatever we split off from in ourselves is allowed no life in the psyche, and what is allowed no life becomes poisonous. This is not the same as "acting out". If we are angry, for example, and dislike the feeling, we can get rid of it in either of two main ways: we can try to avoid it by *repression,* or void it by instantaneous *expression.* But there is a third way: we can simply, even if only for a microsecond, "take it in", that is, feel the anger as an *impression.* This is the way of transformation. The feeling is part of our experience, *an objective and relational fact in our inner world.* If this feeling reality is taken on board along with other psychic facts, such as our thoughts, sensations, images, and so on, and all of these taken together as a whole, then, whether or not we act on the anger, or, indeed, *how* we act on it, which is an ethical decision, becomes closer to a decision made by the person we are as a whole. We know that to say of someone that they have integrity is to acknowledge that they act from a place of (relative) wholeness. This, then, is what falling in love can offer. In general, the dangers inherent in falling in love come from splitting off the parts of ourselves that emerge in the process, and the benefits of the experience come from a willingness to integrate these parts. The attitude we take to these parts is all. If we accept and integrate them, we can begin to experience being "all of a piece".

Further, I want to argue that love itself has the potential to be a creative force that accomplishes this synthesis. *Love itself synthesizes.* A synthesized account that includes the insights from various narratives about passionate love gives us a better (i.e., more complete) picture of this phenomenon. A holistic account of passionate love must also take into account the integrity of the individual as a whole. To put it another way, in order to do justice to the multifaceted phenomenon of falling in love, we must take many narratives into account and without undue bias, while to do justice to the multi-faceted phenomenon that is a human being, we must take into account the many narratives about the human being, also without undue bias. The combination of these two accounts has important implications for how we do therapy. We must be prepared to learn from discourses other than our own and to take these into account, and we must also attempt to see the client as a whole. It also has implications that help us relate better to both our inner and outer figures. Most importantly, it does justice to the potential fullness and richness of the experience of falling in love. As lovers or therapists, we can then better wait with patience for the possibility of love's alchemy working its transformation, even where, or perhaps especially where, this process involves, as it must to a greater or lesser extent, the jealousies, hatred, rages, idealization, denigration, envies, power-plays, sadism, and masochism of shadow material. We will be aware that it can plumb both the best and worst within us. We will be in a better position to co-operate with love's own synthetic tendencies. We will be open to seeing what of value remains when all projections are withdrawn, and we will be prepared to see, in the folly that is falling in love, a possible means for the human being to become who they are.

It only remains for me now to outline a few practical details concerning the process of integration of both outer and inner figures.

Inner integration

Depth psychologies have shown how our relationships with others mirror the relationships we have with our internal figures. If we are to relate well to others, we have to integrate these splintered, split-off aspects of ourselves. Vargiu (1974) describes a process of integration that takes place in five stages. Drawing on dreams and myths as well as practical psychotherapeutic work, I would distinguish six distinct but often overlapping stages that differ somewhat from his. I will here give a short summary of the process as I see it.

Awareness involves simply becoming conscious of the particular fragment of the personality that was hitherto unconscious. The acknowledgement, at this stage, is still at a distance, dissociated: the element is not admitted. One's attitude is likely to be defensive at first, and there can be feelings of aversion; the individual may feel confused, afraid, ashamed, disgusted, bewildered, and disorientated. Even with a positive figure, there may be feelings of shame, inadequacy, and fear, all difficult feelings that might prompt the person into denial of the insight. If, however, the individual does not deny what they see, then the second stage can be reached.

Understanding involves getting to know this element of the psyche. Where the complex appears as a figure from a dream or other imagery, then some kind of dialogue with it is a step towards a better understanding of it. At this stage, we find out what makes the figure tick, how it has come to be this way, what it needs. This process and that of simply giving the part attention can lead to the third stage.

Acceptance is likely to take place with increased knowledge about and understanding of this aspect of oneself. Vargiu (1974) points out that this figure may correlate with certain ideas about what one wants, but these may have been based on believing that these are the only way of getting certain basic needs met. As understanding increases, there begin to emerge some positive feelings. There may be a move from aversion or simple tolerance to attraction. We begin to want to nurture this aspect of ourselves.

Accommodation is the fourth stage, one at which we begin to allow this figure to affect us; we let it in more fully and recognize that we have to change to accommodate it: there is a two-way dialogue and two way relationship.

Integration is the last of the stages that we can actively take. In this stage, any remaining dissociation is dissolved and it is a step involving an entirely new ego position. In a dream, this new perspective is often symbolized by a new landscape. The formerly unconscious aspect is now part and parcel of who we are. It becomes a resource that we can draw upon and our psyche has been enlarged in the process. We are now more than we once were. This leads to the last stage.

Transformation is not a conscious step we can take, but one that now happens autonomously. The individual is no longer the person they once were. The integration of the element creates a "sea change into something rich and strange", as Ariel sings of the drowned prince in Shakespeare's *The Tempest.* It is an alchemical transformation and the whole is more than just the sum of the parts. Since it is instigated by the whole personality (the Self), it is beyond the reach of the ego, and, therefore, always has a miraculous or numinous quality to it.

A good description of each of these stages is given us in the fairytale, "The Frog Prince", in Grimm and Grimm (1812). In the tale, a Princess is playing with a precious golden ball by a spring. She loses it in the water, and is helped to retrieve it by a frog. But the creature demands something of her in return. She is to let him into her house, to let him sit next to her and feed from her plate, and finally to let him into her bed. Hastily, she promises, but, on the retrieval of her ball, she readily forgets her promise. It is only after she fulfils each act that she vouchsafed him that the frog is transformed into a prince. A psychological, Jungian reading of this tale sees the golden ball as a sun symbol, symbol of the Self. It is lost to the Princess, the ego, in the waters of the unconscious, and only a shadow figure from that world can retrieve it for her. But, in order to retrieve our connection with the self, we must integrate the shadow, and this leads to union with the Inner Partner. The rest of the tale gives us an outline of the stages of integration. The stage of *awareness* corresponds to the Princess seeing the frog for the first time when he returns her golden ball and again after she has forgotten all about him and he returns to knock at the palace door. *Understanding* is shown in her recognition, forced upon her by the King's questioning, that she must keep her promise, since the frog is another living being to which she owes an obligation. She and she alone is responsible for him. The stage of *acceptance* is symbolized by letting him into the palace, but she first keeps him at a distance. *Accommodation* is shown by letting him sit next to her and feed from her plate. She must give to this figure and nourish it. Then *integration* is expressed by the Princess taking the frog into her bed. This act hints at sexual union, which is the symbol *par excellence* for integration. The two are united. Finally, we have the breaking of the spell, through a kiss or by throwing the frog against the wall, which is the *transformation*. The frog is a frog no longer, but has become the Prince. He has become a figure of a kindred species to the Princess and also royal, yet, at the same time, he is also a complementary other: a whole and wholly human other.

It is important to note that awareness and understanding are necessary but by no means sufficient. Often, individuals coming to therapy have an expectation that knowing about some complex is enough to be able to rid themselves of it. Once they have gained an intellectual understanding, they can be very disappointed to find that this does not make the difference they had anticipated. The much harder task is for one's feelings to be included, which relates to the stage of acceptance. The inclusion of feelings is a *sine qua non* for full integration to be able to take place. It is the heat, the cooking, which effects the alchemical transformation. But feelings alone are not sufficient either: every therapist knows of people who feel intensely and yet seem caught up in a never-ending repetition of painful dramas. Both the understanding and the feeling are needed for a full transformation to take place.

Outer integration

But we are not only individuals: we also take our place in society, and, as relational psychologies affirm, we become an individual in relationship with others. We need to engage in an analogous process of becoming integrated with others and into society. Adult intimate love, often, but not always, initiated by passionate love, is one of the best arenas in which to learn how this integration can be achieved. Interestingly enough, I think the stages of building a good relationship are very similar to those I have just outlined for the process of integration of inner figures. In order to see the other person as another person in their own right, we first need to become conscious of them as a separate other (awareness); we need to have the interest and curiosity to want to get to know them, to find out who they are and "how they tick" (understanding); we need to accept them as different from us and be able to come to terms with what we do not like, which may involve challenge, but must go beyond denial (acceptance); we need to be able to negotiate the finer details of an everyday relationship, the roughly fifty-fifty, give-and-take of love (accommodation); and, finally, in a relationship between two significant others, if indicated and if all is well, we make the final step of the integration of our separate selves into the sexual and psychological union (not merger) that comprises a couple relationship. This last step effects a transformation of both individuals: each changes because they are in relationship to the other. This part of the story, however, extends beyond the process of falling in love to that of staying in love, and is, therefore, outside of the scope of this book. It is dealt with very thoroughly in Pickering (2008).

Sorting out inner and outer in passionate love relationships

So, it would seem that we have a kind of parallel process occurring between the making of inner and outer relationships, but how do we sort out which is which? When we fall in love, we are often thrown headlong into experiences that have not been that intense since childhood, and in the mêlée of feelings it becomes almost impossible to sort out what is within and what is without. Any analysis, whether in psychotherapy or a process of self-analysis, involves this painstaking sorting out of what is what. We ask ourselves, does my resentment at not being rung by my lover, for example, stem from childhood abandonment experiences? Does my sensitivity to being teased stem from previous bullying? Does my fear of engulfment stem from a suffocating first marriage or perhaps an engulfing mother? There is a process a little like sorting out our computer files: updating them, putting them into useful categories, naming them, and filing them away, but in such a way that we know where to find them again. We also learn how to custom the programmes to fit our particular needs and how to open up the programme options if we need to change the default settings. As we have seen, this near impossible task is described very aptly in the tale of *Amor and Psyche* (Neumann, 1956) in the sorting of the pile of seeds and beans.

Analysis, as Jung points out, is a destructive tool valuable in attacking and destroying pathology. It is like laser treatment that can be used to destroy pathological tissue. For example, in the condition known as macular degeneration, sight is lost due to damaged tissue at the back of the eye. A laser beam can be used to destroy this tissue on the eye retina to improve sight, but if it were used on the healthy retina cells, it would actually *destroy* sight. Thus, what is healthy in a person must, most emphatically, not be subject to analysis. Synthetic processes such as active imagination and elaboration of the material may be of value in its stead.

By completing the painstaking task of sorting out the different elements that can obstruct the path of mature love, we achieve an important step in the process of integration of the various figures, inner or outer. It is important to emphasize again that this is a fractional process: as we integrate inner elements, we will find that we relate better to real outer people; as we learn how to relate better to those others, we find that we relate better to the real inner figures.

All of the fairytales that culminate in the "happily ever after" of a marriage reveal a profound truth: in our inner world we find the same archetypal themes as are to be found in the general and instinctual patterns of behaviour in actual human beings. There is attraction, pair bonding, union, impregnation, birth, the bringing up of progeny, leading to the final letting them out into the world to survive independently in order, perhaps, to repeat the cycle over again for themselves. It is not the dream of the fairy tale romance that is so destructive of human love, but an inability to realize quite what it is telling us. The stories of all our loves, both within and without, lead to the same goal. Falling in love may help us come to the realization that, both internally and externally, "no man is an island entire of itself". There can be no lasting happiness that does not involve the happiness of those objective others within and without the human psyche.

Can we make it happen?

In her chapter, "What do we mean by love?", Claremont de Castillejo (1973) warns that love is not permanent and that we cannot learn to love:

> Love happens. It is a miracle that happens by grace. We have no control over it . . . It comes, it lights our lives, and very often it departs. We can never make it happen nor make it stay . . . We are elected into love. [pp. 116–117]

Yet, given its miraculous nature, it is no surprise that some characters might be tempted to try to control passionate love. Sometimes, that shows itself in an attempt to control the beloved. Jealousy, possessiveness, dominant behaviours, and even submissive ones, can all be means, conscious or unconscious, of controlling love: an attempt to keep it forever, to have it permanently on tap. A hypertrophied will-to-power usurps love–desire.

With our increased understanding of brain states, we have seen how certain feel-good states may have an addictive or near-addictive quality to them. There is a danger that the ego can try to take possession of the experience, seeking to control it rather than wait for it to alight, a visitation from the self. Many addicts of the various addictive substances or actions seem to be susceptible to the desire to use altered states of consciousness as a means of escaping pain. But, perhaps, the "addiction" also reveals to us our deepest need, which is not to perceive ourselves as, nor to live as if we are, an isolated unit, alienated in a meaningless universe, but having had a glimpse of what it is to become absorbed in something beyond ourselves and to experience our self as part of the whole.

A last look at bliss

Behind this desire to control passionate love may be our craving for its bliss. Since this bliss seems to us to come only from without and, in our specific example, only when we are in love, we are doomed to seek again and again the same experience. Then, we are unable to remain faithful to our beloved because the need to re-experience the feelings of being "in love" drives us to fall in love again and again. We do not persevere with the mundane experience of trying to maintain love with the person we have fallen for.

Claremont de Castillejo is right, of course: love is indeed a miracle that happens by grace but, I suggest, only up to a point. She certainly acknowledges that we can perhaps learn to prepare for love. But if, as with mercy, it falls "like a gentle rain from heaven /

Upon the place beneath", there is a great deal more that one can do to help make the most of nature. If I might borrow and extend a metaphor from Teresa of Avila (1979), one can painstakingly irrigate dry land using the water from rain that has filled rivers, or wells, or reservoirs; one can work the land to soften it so that the rain will make an impression in the dried-up soil; one can even build, as is done in the parks of Paris, little miniature dams around the plant to preserve, as in a tiny moat, the precious water around its roots. *In extremis*, as in desert places, one can even engage in a complicated and labour intensive process of desalination of natural seawater. This last might be likened to analysis: an artificial method of construction or reconstruction only indicated where the environment is, or has been, unduly harsh.

We have seen how imagination is one of the greatest tools of transformation, and how evoking love by the creation of "imagined possibilities", using the technique of active imagination (Jung, 1957), is one way of drawing on the fecundity of the past or of creating new possibilities for the future. Working on the shadow, softening resistances to what can suddenly and surprisingly wake us into new growth, is another. And, finally, if or when love does alight in our lives, as with precious rainfall, we can drink it in thirstily and appreciatively, enjoying with gratitude the sheer richness of the experience.

Perhaps compulsion in passionate love comes as a result of a certain laziness that craves the "drug" of bliss without the long, painstaking, and more arduous task of working towards it as a possibility. If that bliss is related to an experience of the ego finding itself lost in something bigger than it, if that is the core of the experience, then we may be able in some way to further this and not remain entirely helpless to the whims of our fate.

I would wish to maintain that the experience of falling in love can give us a perception of the underlying unity within the universe. It gives us a glimpse of what Newberg and d'Aquili (2001) called states of Unitary Being; of a transitional space where the distinctions between self and other, outer and inner, need and gift do not apply. This realm is not attainable only at physical death, as those who understand death only in its concrete form suppose. As Johnson writes (1983), the death here is the death of the ego, its surrender to larger realities.

But these states, by their very nature, are not ones that one can remain in indefinitely. The laundry must be done, a living must be made, and so on. I think the process is best seen as a cyclical movement, a going up the mountain from which a wide perspective is viewed and a going down again in order to see the detail. Fixity in one or other viewpoint perhaps implies a degree of defensive pathology, while the possibility of moving in and out of these two perspectives with a relative degree of freedom indicates health.

As we have seen, falling in love can give us an experience of seeing both the wider perspective and the unique detail, a sense of both the multiplicity and the underlying unity of the universe. It can give us a sense of ourselves as a whole person, all of a piece, and of what it is to love a whole person. We may be called upon to plumb the very depths of our nature and to scale its very heights, to discover both our best and our worst. It is, indeed, true, as Lewis (1960) wrote, that all this is only a glimpse, but it is possible to have a glimpse, and then another, and again another, so that, if we are able to gather together the various threads of the narrative of all our love relationships, those cumulative glimpses may become an insight. Like Parsifal in the story of the Holy Grail (de Troyes, 1991), we may stumble undeserving upon the precious thing our dying world most needs. If we can pause amid our passion and seek the meaning of this experience, then we may yet win our heart's desire.

In its essence, love is more than any feeling; more than sexual attraction or primal instinct; more even than the longing of the soul for the divine. It is all these things and also more. It will always remain ineffable, but, as Eros, it manifests as an indefinable energy that binds our disparate inner selves into a coherent whole, that binds each individual self to society, and that binds humanity to the universe that we inhabit. Through such connection, the tiny part may lose itself only to find itself within the greater whole. For humanity, at least, suffering as it does from an alienation both within and without, this binding is a liberation.

REFERENCES

Andersen, H. C. (1974). *His Classic Fairy Tales*, E. Hangaard (Trans.). London: Book Club Associates [reprinted 1983].

Aristotle (1953). Nichomachaeon ethics. In: J. A. K. Thomson (Trans.), *The Ethics of Aristotle*. London: George Allen & Unwin, 1953 [reprinted London: Penguin Classics, 1975].

Benjamin, J. (1988). *The Bonds of Love*. New York: Random House.

BPD World (2007). *Newsletter*. Issue 2, September. www.bpdworld.org.

Bowlby, J. (1969). *Attachment. Attachment and Loss (Volume 1)*. London: Hogarth Press [reprinted UK: Penguin, 1972].

Bowlby, J. (1973). *Separation: Anxiety and Anger. Attachment and Loss (Volume 2)*. London: Hogarth Press & Institute of Psycho-Analysis [reprinted UK: Penguin, 1975].

Bowlby, J. (1980). *Loss: Sadness and Depression. Attachment and Loss (Volume 3)*. London: Hogarth Press & Institute of Psycho-Analysis [reprinted UK: Penguin, 1991].

Brontë, C. (1847). *Jane Eyre*. London: Smith, Elder & Co.

Brontë, C. (1853). *Villette*. London: Smith, Elder & Co.

Carotenuto, A. (1989). *Eros and Pathos*. Toronto: Inner City Books.

Carroll, R. (n.d.). Love in a scientific climate. http://www.thinkbody.co.uk/papers/Love in a scientific clim.htm.

Claremont de Castillejo, I. (1973). *Knowing Woman*. New York: Putnam [reprinted Shambala, 1990].

Corrigal, J., & Wilkinson, H. (Eds.) (2003). *Revolutionary Connections*. London: Karnac.

d'Aquili, E., & Newberg, A. (2000). The neuropsychology of aesthetic, spiritual, and mystical states. *Zygon, 35*: 39–51.

de Beauvoir, S. (1949). *The Second Sex*. London: Vintage Classics.

de Rougemont, D. (1956). *Love in the Western World*. New York: Pantheon [reprinted Princeton, NJ: Princeton University Press, 1983].

de Troyes, C. (1991). The story of the grail. In: C. Troyes (Ed.), W. Kibbler & C. Carroll (Trans.), *Arthurian Romances*. London: Penguin [reprinted 2005].

Dickens, C. (1859). *A Tale of Two Cities*. London:

Donne, J. (1971) [1635]. Songs and sonnets. In: A. Smith (Ed.), *The Complete English Poems* (pp. 41–92). Harmondsworth: Penguin.

Dourley, J. P. (1987). *Love, Celibacy and the Inner Marriage*. Toronto: Inner City Books.

Duffy, C. (2005). *Rapture*. London: Pan Macmillan.

Edinger, E. (1972). *Ego and Archetype*. New York: Putnam [reprinted Boston, MA: Shambala, 1992].

Evans, M. (2003). *Love: An Unromantic Discussion*. Cambridge: Polity Press.

Fisher, H. (1992). *Anatomy of Love*. New York: Random House [reprinted New York: Ballantine Books, 1994].

Fisher, H. (1994). The nature of romantic love. *The Journal of NH Research, 6*: 59–64.

Fisher, H. (1998). Lust, attraction, and attachment in mammalian reproduction. *Human Nature, 9*: 23–52.

Fisher, H. (2004). *Why We Love: The Nature and Chemistry of Romantic Love*. New York: Henry Holt.

Fisher, H. (2006). The drive to love: the neural mechanism for mate selection. In: R. K. Sternberg & K. Weis (Eds.), *The New Psychology of Love* (pp. 87–115). New York: Yale University Press.

Fisher, H., Aron, A., Mashek, D., Li, H., & Brown, L. (2002). Defining the brain systems of lust, romantic attraction and attachment. *Archives of Sexual Behaviour, 31*: 413–419.

Freud, S. (1905d). *Three Essays in the Theory of Sexuality*. S.E., *7*: 125–245. London: Hogarth.

Freud, S. (1915c). *Instincts and their Vicissitudes*. S.E., *14*: 109–140. London: Hogarth.

Freud, S. (1920g). *Beyond the Pleasure Principle. S.E.*, *18*: 3–64. London: Hogarth.

Gerhardt, S. (2004). *Why Love Matters*. London: Brunner-Routledge [reprinted 2005].

Gilbert, S. M., & Gubar, S. (1979). *The Madwoman in the Attic: The Woman Writer and the Nineteenth Century Literary Imagination*. New York: Yale University Press [reprinted 2000].

Gray, J. (2002). *Men Are from Mars, Women Are from Venus*. London: Harper Element.

Greer, G. (1970). *The Female Eunuch*. London: MacGibbon and Kee.

Grimm, J., & Grimm, W. (1812). *Children's and Household Tales* [reprinted in 2000 as *Household Stories by the Brothers Grimm*. New York: Cosimo].

Guggenbühl-Craig, A. (1977). *Marriage Dead or Alive*. Putnam, CT: Spring.

Heffern, R. (2001). Exploring the biology of religious experience. *National Catholic Reporter*, 20 April.

Hillman, J. (1972). *The Myth of Analysis*. Evanston, IL: Northwestern University Press [reprinted New York: Harper & Row, 1978].

Hilu, V. (Ed.) (1972). *Beloved Prophet: The Love Letters of Kahlil Gibran and Mary Haskel, and her Private Journal*. New York: Knopf.

Hofberg, H. (1890). *Swedish Fairy Tales*, W. H. Myers (Trans.). Chicago, IL: Belford-Clarke.

Hopkins, G. M. (1986). *Gerard Manley Hopkins: The Major Works*. Oxford: Oxford University Press [reprinted 2002].

Hughes, G. J. (2004). Newman and the particularity of conscience. In: I. Ker & T. Merrigan (Eds.), *Newman and Faith* (pp. 53–74). Louvain: Peeter's Press.

Ishiguro, K. (1988). *The Remains of the Day*. New York: Random House [reprinted 1990].

Jacobs, J. (Ed.) (1916). *European Folk and Fairy Tales*. New York: G. P. Putnam's Sons [reprinted Kessinger, 2008].

Johnson, R. A. (1983). *We: Understanding the Psychology of Romantic Love*. New York: Harper & Row.

Jung, C. G. (1954a). Concerning the archetypes, with special reference to the anima concept. In: H. Read, M. Fordham, G. Adler, & W. McGuire (Eds.), R. F. C. Hull (Trans.), *The Collected Works of C. G. Jung*, *9*(i): pp. 54–72 (2nd edn). New York: Princeton University Press.

Jung, C. G. (1954b). *The Practice of Psychotherapy. CW*, *16*.

Jung, C. G. (1956). *Symbols of Transformation*. CW, 5.

Jung, C. G. (1957). The transcendent function. *CW, 8*: 67–91.

Jung, C. G. (1958). A psychological view of conscience. *CW, 10*: 437–455.

Jung, C. G. (1959a). *The Archetypes and the Collective Unconscious. CW, 9*, Part I.

Jung, C. G. (1959b). *Aion. CW, 9*, Part II.

Jung, C. G. (1961). *Memories, Dreams, Reflections*, A. Jaffe (Ed.), C. Winston (Trans.) (3rd edn). London: Random House, 1963.

Jung, C. G. (1971). *Psychological Types*. CW, 6.

Jung, E. (1955). *Animus and Anima*. Zurich. (English paperback edition, New York: Spring, 1985).

Kalsched, D. (1996). *The Inner World of Trauma*. London: Routledge.

Khmara, E. (1985). *Ladyhawke* (story and screenplay). Film directed by Richard Donner.

Klein, M. (1937). Love, guilt and reparation. In: *Love, Guilt and Reparation and Other Works 1921–194* (pp. 306–343). London: Hogarth Press, 1975 [reprinted London: Vintage, 1998].

Klein, M. (1952a). The origins of transference. In: *Envy and Gratitude and Other Works 1946–63* (pp. 48–56). London: Hogarth Press, 1975 [reprinted London: Vintage, 1997].

Klein, M. (1952b). Some theoretical considerations regarding the emotional life of the infant. In: *Envy and Gratitude and Other Works 1946–63* (pp. 61–93). London: Hogarth Press, 1975 [reprinted London: Vintage, 1997].

Klein, M. (1952c). On observing the behaviour of young infants. In: *Envy and Gratitude and Other Works 1946–63* (pp. 94–121). London: Hogarth Press, 1975 [reprinted London: Vintage, 1997].

Klein, M. (1957). Envy and gratitude. In: *Envy and Gratitude and Other Works 1946–63* (pp. 176–235). London: Hogarth Press, 1975 [reprinted London: Vintage, 1997].

Klein, M. (1963). On the sense of loneliness. In: *Envy and Gratitude and Other Works 1946–63* (pp. 300–313). London: Hogarth Press, 1975 [reprinted London: Vintage, 1997].

Langford, W. (1999). *Revolutions of the Heart*. London: Routledge.

Lewis, C. S. (1960). *The Four Loves*. London: Geoffrey Bles [reprinted London: HarperCollins, 1998].

Macdonald, G. (1961). *The Light Princess and Other Fairy Stories*. London: Victor Gollanz [reprinted in *The Complete Fairy Tales*. London: Penguin, 2000].

Mahler, M., Pine, F., & Bergman, A. (1975). *The Psychological Birth of the Human Infant: Symbiosis and Individuation*. New York: Basic Books [reprinted 2000].

Mill, J. S. (1873). As quoted in M. Vernon, in *Church Times*, 5th September, 2008, p. 11.

Neumann, E. (1956). *Amor and Psyche*. Toronto: Princeton University Press [reprinted 1971].

Newberg, A., & d'Aquili, E. (2001). *Why God Won't Go Away*. New York: Random House.

Newberg, A., & Lee, B. (2005). The neuroscientific study of religious and spiritual phenomena: or why god doesn't use biostatistics. *Zygon, 40*: 469–490.

Newberg, A., Alavi, A., Baime, M., Pourdehnad, M., Santanna, J., & d'Aquili, E. (2001). The measurement of regional cerebral blood flow during the complex task of meditation: a preliminary SPECT study. *Psychiatry Research: Neuroimaging Section, 106*: 113–112.

Newberg, A., Pourdehnad, M., Alavi, A., & d'Aquili, E. (2003). Cerebral blood flow during meditative prayer. *Perceptual and Motor Skills, 97*: 625–630.

Nizami (1966). *The Story of Layla and Majnun*, R. Gelpke (Ed. & Trans.). Oxford: Bruno Cassirer [reprinted New Lebanon, NY: Omega, 1997].

Panksepp, J. (1998). *Affective Neruroscience*. Oxford: Oxford University Press.

Person, E. S. (1988). *Dreams of Love and Fateful Encounters*. New York: W. W. Norton [reprinted Arlington, VA: American Psychiatric Association, 2006].

Pickering, J. (2008). *Being in Love*. London: Routledge.

Pounds, N. J. (1994). *The Culture of the English People*. Cambridge: Cambridge University Press.

Pullman, P. (1995). *His Dark Materials Trilogy*. London: Scholastic [reprinted 2008].

Rumi, J. (1984). *Open Secret*, J. Moyne & C. Barks (Trans.). London: Threshold Books [reprinted Boston, MA: Shambala Publications, 1999].

Rumi, J. (1995). *The Essential Rumi* (7th edn), C. Barks (Trans.) New York: HarperCollins [reprinted 1997].

Rumi, J. (1998). *The Love Poems of Rumi*, D. Chopra (Ed.). New York: Harmony Books.

Rumi, J. (1999). *Rumi: Whispers of the Beloved*, M. Mafi & A. M. Kolin (Trans.). London: HarperCollins.

Samuels, A. (Ed.) (1985). *The Father: Contemporary Jungian Perspectives*. London: Free Association Books.

Samuels, A. (1989). *The Plural Psyche*. London: Routledge.

Schisgal, M., & Gelbart, L. (1982). *Tootsie* (screenplay).

Schreiber, F. R. (1973). *Sybil*. New York: Warner Books [reprinted 1995].

Schwartz-Salant, N. (1982). *Narcissism and Character Transformation*. Toronto: Inner City Books [reprinted 1986].

Senese, F. (1998). Anandamide. *General Chemistry Online: The Bliss Molecule*, http://antoine.frostburg.edu/chem/senese/101/features/anandamide.shtml [accessed 23rd September, 2008].

Shaffer, H. J. (2008). What is addiction? A perspective. In: *The Division on Addictions, Cambridge Health Alliance, A Teaching Affiliate of Harvard Medical School*, www.divisiononaddictions.org/html/what isaddiction.htm [accessed 22nd January 2009].

Shah, I. (1982). Fahima and the Prince. In: I. Shah (Ed.), *Seeker after Truth* (pp. 168–170). London: Octagon Press.

Shastri, H. P. (2006). Quoted in Yoga and Love. *Self-Knowledge,* Summer, www.self-knowledge.org/latest/06sum/love.htm [accessed 6th January, 2007].

Smith, M. (Ed.) (1995). *The Letters of Charlotte Brontë, Volume I, 1829–1847*. Oxford: Oxford University Press.

Sondheim, S. (1956). Somewhere. In: *West Side Story*. Amberson Holdings LLC and Stephen Sondheim. Leonard Bernstein Music.

Sullivan, S. (1999). *Falling in Love*. London: Macmillan [reprinted 2000].

Teresa of Avila (1979). *The Interior Castle*, K. Kavanaugh OCD & O. Rodriguez OCD (Trans.). New York: Paulist Press.

Tolkein, J. R. (1968). *The Lord of the Rings Trilogy*. New York: Ballantine.

Vargiu, J. (1974). Subpersonalities. In: J. Vargiu, B. Carter, S. Miller, & S. Vargiu (Eds.), *Synthesis Volume One: The Realization of the Self*. Redwood City, CA: The Psychosynthesis Press, http://www.aap-psychosynthesis.org/resources/articles/subpersonalities.pdf [accessed 14th January, 2009].

von Franz, M. (1970). *An Introduction to The Interpretation of Fairy Tales*. Zurich: Spring [revised edn *The Interpretation of Fairy Tales*. Boston, MA: Shambala, 1996].

von Franz, M. (1974). *Shadow and Evil in Fairy Tales*. Zurich: Spring [reprinted Boston, MA: Shambala, 1995].

von Franz, M. (1977, 1990). *Individuation in Fairy Tales*. Dallas, TX: Spring [revised edition Boston, MA: Shambala, 2001].

von Franz, M. (1997). *Archetypal Patterns in Fairy Tales*. Toronto: Inner City Books.

von Franz, M. (2002). *Animus and Anima in Fairy Tales*. Toronto: Inner City Books.

von Franz, M., & Hillman, J. (1971). *Lectures on Jung's Typology*. New York: Continuum.

Warner, M. (1976). *Alone of all Her Sex: The Myth and Cult of the Virgin Mary*. London: Weidenfeld & Nicolson [reprinted New York: Vintage Books, 1983].

Winnicott, D. W. (1953). Transitional objects and transitional phenomena. In: *Playing and Reality* (pp. 1–25). New York: Tavistock, 1971 [reprinted London: Routledge, 1994].

Winnicott, D. W. (1967). Mirror-role of mother and family in child development. In: *Playing and Reality* (pp. 111–118). New York: Tavistock, 1971 [reprinted London: Routledge, 1994].

Winnicott, D. W. (1971). Playing: creative activity and the search for the self. In: *Playing and Reality* (pp. 53–64). New York: Tavistock, 1971 [reprinted London: Routledge, 1994].

Young-Eisendrath, P. (1997). *Gender and Desire*. College Station, TX: A&M University Press.

Young-Eisendrath, P. (1999). *Women & Desire*. New York: Harmony Books [reprinted New York: Three Rivers Press].

Young-Eisendrath, P., & Hall, J. A. (1991). *Jung's Self Psychology: A Constructivist Perspective*. New York: Guilford Press.